THE LOVELY BONES

By Alice Sebold

Adapted by Bryony Lavery

SAMUEL FRENCH

ISBN 978-0-573-11686-5

www.concordtheatricals.co.uk
www.concordtheatricals.com

This work is published by Samuel French, an imprint of Concord Theatricals.

MUSIC USE NOTE

USE OF COPYRIGHT MUSIC

IMPORTANT BILLING AND CREDIT REQUIREMENTS

FIRST PERFORMANCE

The Lovely Bones was first perfomed at the Royal & Derngate theatre, Northampton in September 2018 with the following cast:

Pete Ashmore	Len Fenerman/Samuel
Charlotte Beaumont	Susie Salmon
Emily Bevan	Abigail Salmon
Bhawna Bhawsar	Ruana Singh/Franny
Susan Bovell	Lynn/Cop/Mrs Flanaghan
Natasha Cottriall	Ruth Connors/Buckley Salmon
Keith Dunphy	Mr Harvey
Karan Gill	Ray Singh/Principal Caden
Jack Sandle	Jack Salmon
Ayoola Smart	Lindsay Salmon

Director	**Melly Still**
Designer	**Ana Inés Jabares-Pita**
Lighting Designer	**Matt Haskins**
Composer	**Dave Price**
Sound Designer	**Helen Skiera**
Movement Director	**Mike Ashcroft**
Assistant Director	**Lucy Bird**

CHARACTERS

ALFIE

RUTH CONNORS

SUSIE SALMON

MR HARVEY

FRANNY

ABIGAIL SALMON

JACK SALMON

LINDSEY SALMON

BUCKLEY SALMON

HOLIDAY – the family dog

RAY SINGH

RUANA SINGH

LEN FENERMAN

PRINCIPAL CADEN

COPS [2]

MRS FLANAGAN

SAMUEL HECKLER

GRANDMA LYNN

GIRL

And dogs in heaven...

And the vanished girls... **FLORA HERNANDEZ, LEAH FOX, WENDY RICHTER** ...

1. We Are in Pieces...

Utter darkness.

Within this...

RUTH *is amazed to see* **SUSIE** *leave earth.*

Somebody's body parts are seen, here and there, in limbo working out how to reassemble...

On earth, in a small town, dismembered and bloody body parts.

HARVEY *gathers up the parts into his sack.*

SUSIE, *reassembles and becomes our helpful hostess...*

2. It Happens

SUSIE My name is Salmon. Like the fish.

Susie.

Fourteen years old.

Favourite quote: *if they give you ruled paper, write the other way.*

Observes **HARVEY** *at his task.*

That's me in there.

December sixth, nineteen seventy-three...

back in the day when people believed things like this didn't happen...

I was murdered

It starts to snow.

She puts on her pom-pom hat that has sewn jingle-bells on it...

I take a shortcut through the cornfield back from junior high.

It's snowing lightly

She sticks out her tongue to catch a snowflake.

A lovely sensation.

Six feet away, **MR HARVEY** *stands.*

HARVEY Don't let me startle you

SUSIE Mr Harvey

HARVEY You're the older Salmon girl, right?

SUSIE Yes

HARVEY How are your folks?

SUSIE Fine.

HARVEY I've built something here

Would you like to see?

SUSIE My mum likes me home before dark

HARVEY It's already after dark, Susie.

Beat.

I've made a little hiding place

SUSIE *(looks around...)* I don't see anything.

HARVEY You should be more observant Susie

He squats down and taps the ground.

Hear that?

A hard non-earth sound.

SUSIE What's that?

HARVEY Wood

It keeps the entrance from collapsing

Other than that...

It's all made out of earth...

SUSIE What is it?

HARVEY Come and see.

And he gets down into the trap...

SUSIE *takes off her jingle-bell hat, curious, she follows him in.*

SUSIE this is *neato*!

(surprised) I haven't said *neato* since elementary school!

HARVEY Look around

She looks around.

it's got a chimney...

shelf for useful stuff...

see...?

SUSIE It's *really* interesting!!!

HARVEY isn't it?

SUSIE I *like* it!

HARVEY it's *warm*

SUSIE How did you *build* it?

HARVEY I made a plan...

and just followed it.

Beat.

Be polite and have a Coke.

Beat.

I'm sure the other kids would.

Beat.

I built this for the neighbourhood kids for a club house...

SUSIE *(She knows he's lying)* right.

it's a *pitiful* lie

She thinks...

She looks at him...

I imagine he's lonely

My father has a nice way of describing people like him...

JACK the man's a *character*, that's all

SUSIE Okay I'll have a Coke

HARVEY Take off your parka

SUSIE Thanks

HARVEY You're very pretty Susie
Do you have a boyfriend?

SUSIE No Mr Harvey...
he's giving me the *skeevies...*
I'll just drink my...

She downs all her Coke in one go.

This is not easy.

HARVEY *watches her drink.*

This is a cool place but I have to go...

The trapdoor shuts.

HARVEY I don't know why you think you're leaving.
Are you a good girl, Susie?
take off your clothes.

Beat.

I want to check you're a virgin.
Parents only want good girls.

FRANNY It's like taking candy from a baby...

SUSIE *leaves her body.*

We hear sounds of **SUSIE** *fighting...*

SUSIE I fight as hard as I can down there
But hard as I can isn't enough.
He begins to shove his hand up under my shirt
I say
"Don't Mr Harvey."
he kisses his wet lips down my face and neck
Please don't.

I feel like a sea in which he stands and pisses and shits.

Don't.

I'm on the ground.

In the ground.

Don't please!

FRANNY Everyone says that before dying.

SUSIE He takes the hat my mother had made me

Smashes it into my mouth

After that the only sound I make is...

Directs us to listen to...

The weak tinkling of bells...

ABIGAIL Susie!

Susie!

Dinner's ready... Jack!

JACK I'll be right there...

ABIGAIL We're having lamb

and string beans...

LINDSEY *(with attitude...) ughstringbeans*

SUSIE he is the pestle

I am the mortar

And **HOLIDAY** *arrives...*

He is whining and begging...

ABIGAIL Lamb's not for *you,* Holiday!

LINDSEY Get *down,* Holiday!

BUCKLEY Mumma!

(as **BUCKLEY** *arrives with...) Look!*

HOLIDAY *circles them...*

They ignore his urgency...

ABIGAIL *(maternal love struggles with art appreciation...)* What a lovely painting, Buckley!!!

JACK Did you do that with your *fingers...*???

ABIGAIL And your *nose*???

BUCKLEY Yes!!

JACK *and* **ABIGAIL** *together enjoy cleaning up the young artist...*

ABIGAIL Susie..?

As she cleans **BUCKLEY**'s *fingers...*

JACK Your brother has a new finger painting!

Beat.

Susie...?

ABIGAIL I made apple crumb cake!

They all sort of wait for **SUSIE** *as...*

The beating of hearts.

Hers like a rabbit.

His a hammer thudding.

SUSIE The dark earth around us smells like...
where worms live

LINDSEY *watches* **HOLIDAY** ...

LINDSEY Holiday what is *wrong* with you...?

HARVEY *(like a lover)* Why don't you get up?

SUSIE When I don't move
he leans to the side
brings back a knife...

I *know* he is going to kill me

He takes the hat from my mouth...

HARVEY Tell me you love me

SUSIE *(gently)* I love you.

The end came anyway.

The trap swings open.

MR HARVEY *drags out, with difficulty, the huge sack and pulls it across earth towards his house as...*

SUSIE *watches until he disappears...*

Thinks about something nicer...

I had been kissed once

by someone I *liked.*

His name was Ray and he was Indian.

Under his yearbook picture

he'd answered the standard

RAY "my heart belongs to...?"

Writes as he says...

"Susie Salmon"

SUSIE I guess *he* had plans too.

RAY *exits.*

Ray... Ray!!!

In his house space, **MR HARVEY** *lowers the sack into his basement...*

HOLIDAY *goes a bit berserk...*

Barking and signalling towards that direction.

LINDSEY Holiday!!!...

shut *up*!!!

3. First Day in Heaven...

Heaven.

FRANNY *stands waiting until...*

SUSIE Why *wasn't* I more observant?
Why didn't I just *observe* my way *out* of there?
I was going to be a wildlife photographer!!!
Why *didn't* I???

FRANNY These questions are fruitless
You didn't and that's that.

She watches **SUSIE**'*s struggle.*

Don't dwell on it.

SUSIE *continues her struggle...*

It does no good.
You're *dead* and you have to *accept* it.

Big one. Teenage frustration and fury.

SUSIE *needs time until...*

SUSIE Who are *you* anyway?

FRANNY I'm Franny.
I'm your intake counsellor.
I manage *all* the junior heavens.
This is *your* heaven.

SUSIE I don't like it!

FRANNY Then *change* it...
It's *your* heaven.
Anything you want you can have.
All you have to do is *desire* it.

It will come...

that's The Deal.

What do you want?

SUSIE *(closes her eyes... We see her wishing... Darkness. A thrumming)* I want to be un-raped and un-killed.

She reaches the boundaries of her heaven...

She's back in the hell of **HARVEY**.

FRANNY That's too far, Susie

SUSIE *shocked and silent.*

You're not ready.

SUSIE *sees* **JACK**.

SUSIE *DAD!!!*

But he cannot hear her now...

JACK *(telephone)* blood type O.

Listens.

pale. her skin's...light I guess...

SUSIE But I'm here

JACK *(Listens. Distinguishing features...?)* regular...

she has this smile...

it's...like stars exploding...

Listens.

Something terrible...

If you've only found a body part...

You can't be certain she's dead

Listens.

No, I know nothing is ever certain.

ABIGAIL *hears this.*

Listens.

Yes, you can come round and get her fingerprints...

HOLIDAY *whines.*

SUSIE There's a *perfect* one on the snow globe in your study, Dad...

JACK *puts the phone down.*

Beat.

Then he takes a full whiskey bottle, contemplates it...

So wants a drink...

But...

Then begins to pour it down the sink...

MUM!

LINDSEY What's that?

JACK Whiskey

LINDSEY Why are you pouring that away?

SUSIE *(sees* **LINDSEY***)* Lindsey...

JACK I'm afraid I might drink it

Beat.

LINDSEY What was the phone call?

JACK What phone call?

LINDSEY the phone call where
You said that thing you *always* say
about Susie's smile...
how "it's like stars exploding."

that phone call

Beat.

It was a cop, wasn't it?

JACK No lies?

LINDSEY No lies

JACK It was a cop.

LINDSEY Tell me.
No lies.
Everything.

JACK The Gilberts' dog found a body part.

Beat.

It might be Susie's.

LINDSEY *flinches.*

He said
Nothing is ever certain

LINDSEY Dad, tell me which body part
Then
I'm going to need to throw up

He gets a metal mixing bowl...

Holds it ready...

HOLIDAY *watches...*

Okay
which body part...

JACK the elbow.

LINDSEY *takes his hand.*

He holds her hand as she throws up.

4. Calling to Earth...

HOLIDAY *barks and yowls to the endless sky.*

SUSIE Holiday!

Seek!

Find!

As **ABIGAIL** *tries to remember what* **SUSIE** *had worn, carried when she last left the house...*

POLICE *and* **TOWNSFOLK** *...searching... a line...*

SUSIE *in line with them while really in her heaven...*

ABIGAIL *(numbly)* Jingle-bell hat

parka/

...Red book bag

Biology book

English book

Jotter...

Charm bracelet

SUSIE Yes...

keep looking...

I'm around somewhere...

eyes down!

look for any traces of me!

Where's the den gone?

It's not here!!!

??????????

He's collapsed the den!

That's *my blood*!

Watches, desperate, uber-teenage-frustration-with-adults until...

COP *(holds up an earth-caked fist...)* Over here!

Muddy copy of To Kill a Mockingbird...

It is examined...

Do they read this at school?

SUSIE/RUTH/RAY *(various)* Yes we do!!!

Us *older* kids!

Sure!

It's on the syllabus!!!

Older kids' syllabus!

Sure!

That's

To Kill a Mockingbird!!!

SUSIE Yes!

I was *carrying* it!

RUTH Mrs Dewitt does a big Shakespeare push right before Christmas

Then she passes out *To Kill a Mockingbird*

SUSIE as a reward

RAY Ask Mrs Dewitt for Susie's paper...

SUSIE/LINDSEY *(a bit proud of...)* "Ostracised: One Man Alone!"

LINDSEY I thought up that title.

SUSIE Credit Hog!

I wrote the thing!!!

Lindsey...?

SUSIE *waits for* **LINDSEY** *to answer back...*

Okay... you also need to
Look for my

SUSIE/RAY ...biology notes from
Mr Botte's class!

RAY/RUTH That was our last lesson before...

SUSIE Dig!

FENERMAN Okay... We'll check this out...
okay...
look for...
school stuff...
papers
text books
notes whatever/ anything...

SUSIE Try *the green-painted* house
look!
close to my parents!!!
There! See????
Mr Harvey's
He's got most of me in his basement!!!
Check *his* fingerprints!!!

But the police exit...

HARVEY *appears, watching...*

Him!

Terrible impotence of...

Just WATCHING!!!
This is making me *crazy*!

Sees **ABIGAIL** *...*

Mum!

ABIGAIL *passes* **HARVEY** …

HARVEY Mrs Salmon

ABIGAIL Mr Harvey

HARVEY I heard about the horrible, horrible tragedy.

ABIGAIL *can't speak. Just nods.*

What was your daughter's name, again?

ABIGAIL/SUSIE Susie

SUSIE You *know* that!

You *called* me Susie!

HARVEY I hope they get the bastard.

I'm sorry for your loss.

SUSIE Mum...

I'm in *heaven*

It's *horrible*!!!

He's the one who...

But **ABIGAIL** *exits as...*

FRANNY *arrives...*

The man has NO SHAME!!!

FRANNY you can't expect *shame*

SUSIE He *knows* my name!

FRANNY Exactly.

SUSIE *is desperate.*

Calm/ down.

SUSIE Don't tell me what to do, *you're* not my *mum*

ABIGAIL *alone, smoking...*

I want to talk to my *mum*

FRANNY Talk all you want she won't hear

SUSIE *MUM!!!*

I want Mum.

FRANNY Can't have her...

You know the score.

Beat.

What do you want that you can *have*???

All you have to do is

FRANNY/SUSIE desire it

If you desire it enough

FRANNY And understand *why*

Really *know*

FRANNY/SUSIE It Will Come...

SUSIE *defiantly wishes for and gets...*

Multiple telephones.

SUSIE Calling all cops...

This is *Susie Salmon*!!!

Try the *green* house close to my parents!!!

Mr Harvey's

He's got most of me *in his basement*!!!

But, no one hears.

It doesn't *work*!!!

FRANNY All you have to do is...

SUSIE I *know...*

SUSIE *wishes.*

do you mind...?

this is private type thing.

FRANNY, *who gets, if not appreciates teenagers, gives her space...*

Desires... a song in the style of ***"YOU MAKE ME FEEL BRAND NEW"*** *by The Stylistics plays* as...*

RAY *appears, Soul Train Love God as...*

He helped me cheat on my algebra exam

He kissed me by my locker

His lips were chapped

We had *plans*

(calls) Franny!

I *know* what I want...

I want to *grow up...*

FRANNY People grow up by *living*

SUSIE I want to *live*

FRANNY You can't

SUSIE I want Mr Harvey *dead* and me *living*! *Don't tell me*

FRANNY/SUSIE That's out

That's the deal.

SUSIE There isn't a lot of *bullshit* in *my* heaven.

FRANNY *exits...*

And **SUSIE** *watches as...*

---

* A licence to produce THE LOVELY BONES does not include a performance licence for "YOU MAKE ME FEEL BRAND NEW". The publisher and author suggest that the licensee contact PRS to ascertain the music publisher and contact such music publisher to license or acquire permission for performance of the song. If a licence or permission is unattainable for "YOU MAKE ME FEEL BRAND NEW", the licensee may not use the song in THE LOVELY BONES but should create an original composition in a similar style or use a similar song in the public domain. For further information, please see Music Use Note on page iii.

5. A Suspect...

BUCKLEY/LINDSEY *making Christmas cards...*

LINDSEY That's nice.

Pointing.

What's *that,* Buckley...?

BUCKLEY That's the In-between.

?

Beat.

Where's Susie...?

LINDSEY *(beat)* Out.

Beat.

Want me to help?

BUCKLEY No.

I want Mum to help.

JACK *taking* **HOLIDAY** *for a walk...*

ABIGAIL *listlessly bringing home presents...*

A tree...

They untangle, carefully...

As...

COP Detective Fenerman...

Sir...

look here...

bird's nest

see...?

something
among the leaves and twigs...?

FENERMAN shreds of paper...

SUSIE my *biology* stuff...
from Mr Botte's class...

They examine...

To them...

COP some handwriting on it...

FENERMAN *(...)* That's not *her* handwriting/...

SUSIE That's not *my* handwriting...

FENERMAN Dear Susie
Desdemona is nothing compared to you...
"Perdition Catch my Soul...
but I do love /thee Susie Salmon..."

SUSIE ...don't read it it's *private*!!!

But they do...

COP Signed "The Moor"

SUSIE It's on his mother's *special* rice paper...

FENERMAN Who's "The Moor?"

SUSIE It's a *love* note

COP The brown kid
with the la-di-da accent

FENERMAN Ray Singh

Another nearby space... another family...

RAY SINGH, *his* **MOTHER, RUANA SINGH,** *safeguarding her son...* **COP** *...and* **FENERMAN** *...*

RUANA Ray is not feeling well

FENERMAN Sorry to hear that Ma'am.

COP Why are you not feeling well, young man?

Is there something you want to get off your chest, son?

Beat.

RAY Okay…

Yes I *did* write Susie Salmon this note

FENERMAN this note… seems like a bit of a *love* note…

RAY *Yes*, it's a love note.

Yes, I put it in her notebook after Mr Botte asked her tc collect the pop quiz

Yes I called myself *the Moor…*

Because…

He indicates his skin colour.

We'd been doing *Othello…*

RAY *storms off as…*

JACK Ray Singh

ABIGAIL Why are the police speaking to that sweet boy?

LINDSEY Ray Singh is up for *Gifted.*

Ray Singh is *nice.*

SUSIE We *all* know it's *not* Ray Singh.!!!

FENERMAN Your son wasn't in school, ma'am,

when the girl disappeared

RUANA *(lights cigarette…)* What day did this girl disappear?

FENERMAN The sixth…

RUANA *(inhales and smiles…)* Officers…

Despite his *darker skin…*

Which must *obviously* make him *suspect* to *you*...
you should be aware
his father teaches post-colonial history at Penn...
and on December *sixth*...
Ray was *with* his father
at International House...
representing the *teenage* viewpoint at
"Suburbia: The American Experience" ...
so... you will discover... if you investigate just a *bit* further...
that
Ray has a whole *host* of nations to testify on his behalf...

6. It's a Murder Inquiry...

FENERMAN *and a* **COP**, *Salmon house...* **ABIGAIL, JACK** *central,* **HOLIDAY** *suspicious,* **BUCKLEY** *somewhere nearish, drawing...* **LINDSEY** *peripheral, eavesdropping...*

FENERMAN We've found a personal item.

We think it's Susie's

Both parents go still.

Then...

ABIGAIL What?

FENERMAN *holds out an evidence bag... in it, the pom-pom hat...*

LINDSEY Her jingle-bell hat.

FENERMAN We've tested the fibres.

It was used during the crime

JACK What?

FENERMAN We think...

possibly... as a way to keep her quiet

JACK What?

FENERMAN there are traces of saliva.

COP He probably gagged her with it...

Beat.

ABIGAIL *and* **JACK** *look at each other.*

FENERMAN Mr Salmon...

With the amount of blood we've found...

And the violence I'm afraid it implies...

And the other material evidence

We must work with the assumption that your daughter has been killed.

ABIGAIL *and* **JACK** *...two separate reactions... she sort of almost nods... he sort of almost shakes his head...*

We'll be working this as a murder investigation from this point on...

JACK But there's no body

FENERMAN I'm very sorry.

FENERMAN *exits.*

JACK *(to* **ABIGAIL***)* But there's no body.

ABIGAIL *looks at him.*

He tries to touch her.

She pulls away.

Scene dissolves... **LINDSEY** *straight to...*

7. Strategies for Coping 1...

LINDSEY*'s bedroom...*

SUSIE *and* **LINDSEY** *immediately to...*

BOTH Curl the edges of yourself up and fold them under where no one can see

until you are small and hard like a stone

They do.

Stay still as long as you can

They do.

Take deep breaths.

They do.

Hold them

They do.

Then...

get strong to go back and face...

8. Principal Caden Does Good...

PRINCIPAL'*s office...*

SUSIE/LINDSEY *(stereo loathing)* Principal Caden

PRINCIPAL CADEN At *our* school

Your *principal* is your *pal* with principles!

SUSIE/LINDSEY Yes Principal Caden.

PRINCIPAL CADEN Lindsey

I'm sorry to hear of your loss

LINDSEY What exactly is my loss?

PRINCIPAL CADEN Sit in the "Talking Chair", Lindsey.

We're here to help in any way we can

LINDSEY *(offers him nothing)* I see you're *reading.*

Good.

Curriculum?

May I?

Reluctantly, she shows him.

PRINCIPAL CADEN *(he reads)* "Erica *(soft Y)* Jong...

(teenage contempt) Jong

PRINCIPAL CADEN ...Fear of Flying"

Then.

... "Albert Camus *(wrong pronunciation)*

LINDSEY *(huger teenage contempt)* Al-berre Cam-oo

PRINCIPAL CADEN *The Rebel...*"

PRINCIPAL CADEN *hasn't heard of them.*

LINDSEY *offers him nothing.*

Would you like to talk about it?

LINDSEY What?

PRINCIPAL CADEN Your loss

LINDSEY I wasn't aware I had lost anything.

SUSIE Make her *laugh*!

Sit on *a fart* cushion!

PRINCIPAL CADEN You're the only Salmon girl now... so...

SUSIE No I'm still here.

FRANNY You're not.

PRINCIPAL CADEN Mr Dewitt is considering coaching a girls team

He's watched how you are as competitive as his boys...

SUSIE Because, Principal *Hopeless* she's clever and/gifted and...

PRINCIPAL CADEN He thinks *other* girls would come out for soccer if *you* led the charge

What do you say?

LINDSEY I'd say it would be pretty hard to play soccer

On the soccer field when it's approximately twenty feet from where my sister was supposedly murdered

SUSIE *(celebratory body and raised arms...) Score!*

LINDSEY Anything else?

Beat.

I'm late for first period.

PRINCIPAL CADEN I'm putting you forward for Gifted Camp, Lindsey...

You and Ruth Connors and Samuel Heckler and Ray Singh...

All My Smartest Seniors!

SUSIE From *my* Year!

Wow, Little Sis!!!

PRINCIPAL CADEN Think about it.

Let me know if you want me to sign you up.

SUSIE You made *Gifted,* Lindsey!

Wow!

9. Strategies for Coping 2

LINDSEY *bedroom.*

LINDSEY *lies on floor... ten sets of sit-ups.*

Then, ten Marine head-up ones and push-ups.

Then, two very heavy-book bicep curls as...

10. Ruth...

SUSIE On my way out of earth

I touched *Ruth Connors...*

RUTH *is on earth as...*

SUSIE *reenacts as...*

She was in my way

As I shrieked out of life...

RUTH *(telling a very sceptical* **FENERMAN**) I was standing near Mr Botte's *red Fiat...*

Suddenly

Down out of the soccer field

I saw this pale running ghost

Coming toward me

FENERMAN *(taking notes)* ghost

SUSIE Me!

RUTH It was *female*

I could *sense* that

It flew *up* out of the field

Its eyes were *hollow*

FENERMAN hollow eyes

SUSIE *No they weren't!*

RUTH *drives* **SUSIE** *crazy. Not friends...*

RUTH It had a thin white veil over its body

As light as cheesecloth

FENERMAN cheesecloth

SUSIE *No I didn't!*

(explanatory...) Ruth writes *poetry...*

RUTH I could see its face coming up through it

The nose

The eyes

The face, the hair

FENERMAN *gently closes his notebook as...*

SUSIE Ruth

You're letting your *imagination* get in the way of *fact*...

RUTH *shivers delicately...*

But

You *saw* me

Ruth...

Ruth!! Go round and see my parents!

RUTH *impervious...*

Tell them!

No movement...

Go look for *clues*

Still no movement...

I was wearing my *very distinctive* silver charm bracelet...

She clutches her wrist.

It is not there.

Where is it?????

RUTH *seems to be about to...*

Go find it, Ruth!!!

But she...

RUTH I'm going to write a poem about it...

probably...a *villanelle*...

RUTH *exits.*

SUSIE *is beyond exasperated...*

SUSIE desire something *simple...*

And wishes hard...

DOGS!!! *Dancing dogs!!!*

Dogs fill her heaven.

HOLIDAY, *on earth, seems to sense them and wails as the moon rises...*

You dogs don't shut down your desire to *know,* do you?

Dogs look helpful...

just because the smell is *bad*

or the object is *dangerous*

Do you?

They agree that they don't.

No, you don't

They humour her.

You *hunt.*

Don't you?

Dogs look willing to do whatever she is saying even though...

You haven't *a clue* what I'm saying have you, Dogs?

Dogs agree they haven't a clue what she is saying...

Hunt, Susie!!!

Dogs doggily applaud her choice.

11. Breaking Through...

JACK *looking at* **SUSIE***'s snowglobe...*

BUCKLEY *nearby, sleeping.*

SUSIE Inside the snow globe in my father's study
there was a penguin wearing a red and white striped scarf...
he would turn it over
let all the snow collect at the top
then invert it
and I'd...

Into memory.

She touches the snow globe with her index finger.

Daddy...?
the penguin's all alone in there...

JACK Don't worry

SUSIE Why not, Dad?

JACK Look at his face.

SUSIE He's smiling.

JACK he has a nice life
he's trapped in a perfect world.

Out of memory.

SUSIE My baby
Remember this?

Handles it tenderly, then...

He smashes it into the mirror.

BUCKLEY *stirs.*

Dad!

Snow starts to fall.

BUCKLEY *stirs.*

Dad... *No!!!*

Without knowing *how*...

I reveal myself

She is reflected in every shard and sliver...

Just for a second

Then I'm gone

Her image disappears.

BUCKLEY Daddy...

Are you alright...?

JACK *(is quiet for a while)* I *saw* you!!!

Then...

He laughs.

Let me see you again!!!

He is about to smash the mirror but...

BUCKLEY *(in the doorway... holding on to the doorknob...)* Daddy?

Are you okay?

JACK Yes Buckley

Daddy just... broke something.

BUCKLEY *(picks up penguin from broken snow globe)* Penguin

JACK *(wraps him in his arms)* You are so special to me, little man.

I will see that...

Rocks him with…

You will be a *king*

a *doctor*

a *wildlife photographer*

BUCKLEY That's *Susie,* Daddy…

JACK Susie the wildlife photographer

Buckley the whatever you like

BUCKLEY the *Superhero*

JACK anything you dream you can be…

BUCKLEY *snuggles up next to* **SUSIE**.

JACK *performs the floating sheet game over both of them as…*

Who are you?

Where did you come from?

SUSIE *kisses* **BUCKLEY**'*s cheek.*

He lightly brushes that spot.

SUSIE The truth is very different from what we learned at school.

The truth is

The line between the living and the dead

Can

It seems

Be blurred…

how?

we just both remembered me touching the snow globe *at the same time*

didn't we, Daddy…?

Mum…?

That photo!

Remember???

SUSIE *finds her mother in* **SUSIE***'s room.*

ABIGAIL *has a photograph in her hand.*

SUSIE *and* **ABIGAIL** *look together at the photograph...*

Into memory.

At only eleven years old...

Susie Salmon

budding but brilliant wildlife photographer

with her birthday camera...

captures this strange wild woman

Click from a camera.

It captures an unhappy earlier **ABIGAIL**.

To herself.

Mum...?

ABIGAIL *out of reverie.*

Happy Birthday Future Wildlife Photographer!!!

I just caught you in your natural environment like in *National Geographic...*

ABIGAIL Oh Susie

this isn't my natural environment.

I got brought here to this alien place by your father.

I'm really a wild wild Amazon.

Out of memory.

ABIGAIL *stops smiling.*

Looks up from the photograph…

What am I doing here?

ABIGAIL *walks away from the photograph to smoke or something…*

BUCKLEY *follows…*

BUCKLEY Mummy…

…Mummy?

SUSIE *Mum!!!*

She watches her mother suffering.

FRANNY You're shivering

SUSIE *(proves this as…)* I just want to be down *there* with *them*

FRANNY *(gently)* that's

SUSIE *out*

I know…

So… **SUSIE** *wishes for…*

And gets…

12. Secret Signals to the World...

A song in the style of ***"SPACE ODDITY"*** **by David Bowie plays.*

SUSIE Help me, David...

FRANNY *(attitude)* Gee...

try it.

I'm going to listen to some Rachmaninov...

Exits.

The music spreads and fills **SUSIE***'s heaven.*

She floats like Major Tom.

On earth, distant, **HOLIDAY** *barks.*

SUSIE *remembers...*

The vinyl scratches.

SUSIE Dog, elbow.

You *forgot* my *elbow*

you're not as fastidious as you like to think you are, Mr Harvey...

HARVEY *is with his sack and its contents...*

I mean...*cloth* sack for a *bloody* body...

I'm seeping out of the bag!

---

* A licence to produce THE LOVELY BONES does not include a performance licence for "SPACE ODDITY". The publisher and author suggest that the licensee contact PRS to ascertain the music publisher and contact such music publisher to license or acquire permission for performance of the song. If a licence or permission is unattainable for "SPACE ODDITY", the licensee may not use the song in THE LOVELY BONES but should create an original composition in a similar style or use a similar song in the public domain. For further information, please see Music Use Note on page iii.

Lovely hopeful discovery...

HARVEY make a plan...

SUSIE make a mistake

make a *mistake* Mr Harvey

HARVEY ...and *stick* to it!

if you are going to *succeed*

never use an old pattern...

SUSIE *old* pattern?

HARVEY you watched the weather...

Looks at the sky...

you acted during light to heavy precipitation... so

you robbed the police of evidence!!!

He smiles.

you make each kill a surprise, George Harvey

SUSIE *(realises...)* I'm not the first girl you've killed, am I?!!!???

HARVEY and then you get to keep something back for yourself...

to remind you...

SUSIE the knife... keep the *knife...*

HARVEY you

SUSIE Make a mistake, Mr Harvey

HARVEY *(examines the bloody knife)* I'll keep *you*!

SUSIE *yes!!!*

Don't wash off my blood, Mr Harvey...

It starts to snow.

HARVEY ah...*snow... (He's thrilled at the snow as he manhandles the sack into the safe.)*

A house should be spotless and *fragrant.*

If people *call*

it should be *immaculate*

and you should be clear and calm

SUSIE We've left a stain haven't we, Mr Harvey?

HARVEY *(Sees the stain. Rubs the stain. It's dry.)* It's okay

it's fine

it looks like oil.

Carries the safe off as…

SUSIE Where are you taking me?

…

HARVEY The sinkhole

SUSIE …where we *dump stuff*?

MR HARVEY *plays carols on his car radio…*

MRS FLANAGAN Good evening.

Got an item?

HARVEY Yep. Twenty dollars?

Hands her a twenty dollar bill…

MRS FLANAGAN *watches him struggle…*

MRS FLANAGAN *Heavy!*

What you got in there, a dead body?

MRS FLANAGAN *and* **HARVEY** *smile…*

SUSIE It's not funny!

HARVEY Old safe of my father's

Finally got it out here

Been meaning to do it for years.

MRS FLANAGAN Does it open?

HARVEY No one remembers the combination

MRS FLANAGAN Anything in it?

HARVEY Stale air.

HARVEY *is still struggling...*

MRS FLANAGAN You need any help?

HARVEY That would be lovely

They manhandle the safe, drop it in the sinkhole.

They watch it sink.

MRS FLANAGAN There she goes

HARVEY There she goes!

SUSIE There I go! Safe from the moles. At least.

MRS FLANAGAN Merry Christmas.

And exits...

HARVEY Merry Christmas

HARVEY *listens to the radio still playing in his car. Stands looking at the sinkhole.*

Sings along to a Christmas song in the style of ***"SANTA CLAUS IS COMIN' TO TOWN"*****.*

Puts his cold hands in his pockets...

Retrieves...

SUSIE*'s silver charm bracelet...*

---

* A licence to produce THE LOVELY BONES does not include a performance licence for "SANTA CLAUS IS COMIN' TO TOWN". The publisher and author suggest that the licensee contact PRS to ascertain the music publisher and contact such music publisher to license or acquire permission for performance of the song. If a licence or permission is unattainable for "SANTA CLAUS IS COMIN' TO TOWN", the licensee may not use the song in THE LOVELY BONES but should create an original composition in a similar style or use a similar song in the public domain. For further information, please see Music Use Note on page iii.

SUSIE My charm bracelet!

You kept it!

Ticks off... as he fondles...

House

Pennsylvania keystone

Ballet slipper

Thimble

Bicycle...

SUSIE *stands with him.*

Sky on earth is dark blue...

Mr Harvey can see for miles

I'm going to stand with him

Go where he will go

Be there when he makes a mistake

The snow has stopped

There's wind

MR HARVEY *takes the Pennsylvania keystone.*

The Pennsylvania keystone...

That's engraved with my initials!!!

My *dad* did that.

Keep that keystone close, Mr Harvey!!!

He examines the rest of the bracelet...

My favourite is *the bike*

HARVEY *throws the rest of the bracelet, with the bike. into the sinkhole.*

it's got *working* wheels...!!!

HARVEY *puts the keystone in his pocket.*

Merry Christmas, *Mr* Harvey

13. Wrapping...

ABIGAIL *wrapping family presents...*

JACK *arrives, buzzing, with brand new leather gloves.*

JACK We need to wrap these!

ABIGAIL These were for *Susie*

HOLIDAY *barks.*

JACK They're *still f*or Susie!
She needs warm hands wherever she is!!!

ABIGAIL *wraps the leather gloves for her mad husband...*

BUCKLEY Will Santa Claus bring me some *building bricks*?

LINDSEY Only if you stop asking every minute?

JACK *goes to the window, watches,* **HOLIDAY** *barks as...*

JACK Mr Harvey's in his garden.
In the snow.
With a book!

JACK *watches him from his house...*

HOLIDAY *growls.*

SUSIE Yes Holiday! Tell them!

LINDSEY Buckley, I'm sorry

JACK *joins* **HARVEY** *in the garden.*

HOLIDAY *whimpers.*

BUCKLEY *takes his place at the window and watches them both...*

14. A Mat Tent...

HARVEY *in his back garden... a book about the Dogon and Bambara of Mali...*

Starts, with reference to it, assembling stuff for a frame as...

JACK What's this?

JACK *joins* **MR HARVEY.**

What's this?

MR HARVEY A mat tent.

He continues erecting the structure as...

I like to *build*

Fetching stuff...

experiment with *structures...*

Continues as...

I've been reading this book...about the Dogon and Bambara of Mali...the Immezzureg tribe...

They make these tents...as part of their preparation

for *marriage...*

the bride sits in the tent

and the groom

visits her

when they are to be *joined*

so...

it's sort of...*ceremonial...*

Stops and...

Mr Salmon, I'm sorry for your loss

JACK Thank you.

Beat.

MR HARVEY Do you want to help?

JACK Sure *(and they start to work together erecting a strange tent...)*

MR HARVEY The Immezzureg tribe

of course

use *natural* poles

branches of trees

(that corner right there)

stuff grown in *the earth*

...

they

lash the *arch* pieces on to pronged posts

JACK Okay

MR HARVEY Then they *weave* more slender rods through the pieces to form *semi*-arches

JACK Okay

SUSIE *is in the rods and poles...*

HARVEY when the tent is ready

for the newly married man and wife...

the women make the sheet that covers it

as beautiful as possible...

Beat.

this is sort of for my *wife* Sophie

she died...

SUSIE You mean *me*

JACK I'm sorry

HARVEY it's snowing

JACK so it is...

MR HARVEY I need to do something in my house...

JACK Okay

HARVEY *heads for...*

JACK *looks up at the snow.*

snow...
I can *hear* you, honey
what is it?

SUSIE Dad
He's not making a cup of tea

In his house, **MR HARVEY** *moves his sketchbook...*

Gets a crumpled paper sack.

Looks in it.

Dad
He's checking on his *knife...*

HARVEY *gets out the bloody knife.*

my *blood* is on his knife
his *fingerprints* are on the knife

JACK did anyone ask this man where he was
the day you disappeared?

SUSIE That *black* on *the blade*

JACK did anyone *see* him in the cornfield?

SUSIE That's my *blood...*
if you just went in his house you'd *catch* him!!!

Send Dad a sign!

His favourite flower!!!

Concentrate!

She concentrates hard.

In heaven space... **FRANNY** *sees, in heaven, geranium petals swirl.*

FRANNY *Geraniums?*

Watches **SUSIE** *watching earth...*

SUSIE Not in HEAVEN!!! *HERE!!!*

FRANNY Susie...*what are you doing??*

SUSIE Helping Dad trap him.

JACK *suddenly looks towards the direction of* **HARVEY***'s house.*

Go In His House, Dad!!!

But **HARVEY** *returns with white cotton sheets.*

JACK What are those for?

HARVEY Tarps

Their hands... **JACK, SUSIE, HARVEY** *touch.*

Electric shock effect.

JACK You know something.

They stare at each other.

Snow falls heavier.

JACK *moves towards* **HARVEY.**

HARVEY That's enough now.

Why don't you go home?

JACK *(whispers:)* Susie

HARVEY We're building a tent.

The neighbours saw us.

We're friends now.

JACK You *know* something

HARVEY Go home.

I can't help you.

15. Irrational...

ABIGAIL Jack...this is *crazy*...the cops *must* have checked/ him out...

JACK Is he a drinker? he's got kind of bloodshot eyes...

and he *shakes...*

I think if he's a drinker...

ABIGAIL I don't think he's a /

JACK we could invite him over...get him *drunk*...maybe *he's a talker...*

ABIGAIL He's *really* not a talker Jack we shouldn't...

JACK I think Susie watches me...

SUSIE *(in heaven, is ecstatic...)* Dad... I *do!*

ABIGAIL Jack...that's...

JACK I wasn't there when she needed me...

SUSIE Dad...

HOLIDAY *upsets* **BUCKLEY***'s building bricks...*

BUCKLEY You Dumb Dog!!!

HOLIDAY *whimpers and runs off.*

LINDSEY *runs for her bedroom.*

JACK Lindsey

LINDSEY go away

JACK Honey

LINDSEY Go away

He doesn't.

What?

JACK I want to know how you *are*

LINDSEY I want to be *alone*

JACK I'm here if you need me.

LINDSEY I'm handling this *alone*

Exits...

FENERMAN *joins them...*

JACK I don't want to sound irrational, Detective Fenerman

FENERMAN Len, please

ABIGAIL Len

JACK *Harvey...*
I'm certain he *knows* something...
I helped him build that crazy *tent...*
look how close his house is to the *cornfield...*

FENERMAN I'll check it out.

JACK I *know* there's something *off about* him...
where *was* /he at the...

FENERMAN Jack, I'll check him out.
Don't talk to anyone.

To **ABIGAIL.**

Don't let him talk to anyone

To **JACK.**

...And don't approach him again.

To **ABIGAIL.**

keep an eye on him
he mustn't approach him again.
Okay?

ABIGAIL Okay.

FENERMAN *exits one way,* **ABIGAIL** *another...* **JACK** *follows* **ABIGAIL** ...

JACK He *knows* something, Abigail...

She's gone.

Abigail...

he knows something...

BUCKLEY Mumma

Mumma?

ABIGAIL Stop.

Everybody *stop*

BUCKLEY Mumma... Where's Susie?

JACK Buckley...

Did you put away your game?

BUCKLEY What's wrong with Mummy?

HARVEY *space...*

HARVEY Mr Salmon was on one of his *walks.*

FENERMAN Walks?

HARVEY The poor man's *always* walking...

And he helped me build my bridal tent

FENERMAN *Bridal* tent?

HARVEY Each year

I do it for *Leah.*

My *wife.*

I'm a *widower*

FENERMAN I'm sorry I didn't know that

HARVEY I was trying

this *mourning* ritual I learned from reading about the nomad tribes in Mali...

when a wife dies

they recreate the bridal tent...

SUSIE *(to* **FENERMAN**...*)* He's lying

HARVEY Christmas is a bad time for us bereaved.

FENERMAN I know.

HARVEY It seemed to *help* my *grief* somehow...

SUSIE Liar!!!

FENERMAN Okay.

HARVEY Detective Fenerman...

I feel *terrible* about what happened to that girl.

I tried to *express* that to Mr Salmon.

I *know* from experience nothing makes sense at a time like this...

FENERMAN So... Mr Harvey

you do this thing every year?

HARVEY yes

FENERMAN You erect a *tent* every year?

HARVEY yes

FENERMAN on this same spot...?

SUSIE Got him he's never /built one there before!!!

HARVEY *(beat)* Ah...no!

In the *past* I've done it *inside*

But

This year...

we married in *winter* you see...

so

I thought...try it *outside...*

In the snow...

My wife Leah just *loved* snow

SUSIE Liar

HARVEY I normally do it in my basement

where I have all Leah's things.

Detective...do you need to check it out...?

SUSIE *Yes we Do!!!*

HARVEY It's a sort of *shrine* to her.

SUSIE *Liar!*

Beat.

Come on!

Beat.

There's *evidence* there!!!

FENERMAN No.

It's okay.

HARVEY You're welcome to look...

FENERMAN It's okay.

SUSIE *Aaaaarghhhhh!!!*

FRANNY *appears. Watches* **SUSIE.**

HARVEY How's your investigation coming?

Finding anything?

FENERMAN Clues find their way in good time

SUSIE Its *time!!!*

FRANNY Susie...this is *out.*

FENERMAN *to* **SALMON** *house space...*

FENERMAN He's certainly a bit *tweaked at an angle*

But I've nothing on him.

JACK What did he say about *the tent*?

FENERMAN Built it for his wife.

Leah

JACK His wife is called *Sophie*

FENERMAN Nope.

Leah.

I wrote it down.

JACK Abigail!

He told me *Sophie*!

Mrs Stead told *you* his wife's name was Sophie!

ABIGAIL I don't remember, Jack.

JACK At the *block/ party*!!!

ABIGAIL I don't remember, Jack.

JACK So where did I get *Sophie*? Where?

From *somewhere*!!!

FENERMAN *exits as...*

SUSIE Why didn't you check his basement out?????

He pretends he has a dead wife and he gets a free pass???

JACK Abigail...

Leah?

Sophie?

His wife has *two* completely different names!!!

ABIGAIL Jack...

JACK He's *scared* he's making *mistakes* he's making things *up* how do we get him to...

Remembers.

Get him drunk I need to get him drunk...

He's a *talker* he talked to *me* he talked to *Fenerman...*

SUSIE Dad *knows*!

He *knows*!!!

Mum...he *knows*!!

JACK Abigail...

ABIGAIL Jack, it's *Christmas.*

16. Christmas Day

A terrible Christmas Day in the Salmon house...

BUCKLEY *has some building logs.*

HOLIDAY *tries to murder his squeaky toy...*

ABIGAIL, *nothing. She is drinking an eggnog.*

It is all terrible...

JACK *and* **ABIGAIL** *drink eggnog, watch* **BUCKLEY** *assemble his logs...*

BUCKLEY I was building *a home.*

Everybody watches him.

LINDSEY Holiday, shut *up.*

He doesn't.

BUCKLEY Where's Susie?

They look down.

Where's *her* presents?

Beat.

Then...

LINDSEY *(with gloves...)* Here they are.

They all look at them.

Eventually...

LINDSEY *takes the gloves.*

Come on Holiday...

let's go for a walk...

HOLIDAY *barks excitedly.*

LINDSEY *takes the gloves to the cornfield.*

HOLIDAY *watches with interest...*

In heaven **FRANNY** *watches* **SUSIE** *mope...*

FRANNY Merry Christmas, Susie.

SUSIE *(unhappy)* Merry Christmas

FRANNY If you want something hard enough...

SUSIE I *know*!

Beat.

How did *you* get here?

FRANNY I was a social worker for the homeless and destitute...

SUSIE *(of course she was!) ...right*

FRANNY A very angry man came
looking for his wife
I got between them...
he shot me in the face

Does the gun action...

Does her face exploding.

SUSIE Wow.
That's sort of cool, I guess...

FRANNY I *chose* to serve...
I *still* choose to serve
I *like serving...*
that's *my* heaven...
That's *my* David Bowie
If you need me... *(and exits)*

LINDSEY You got some Gloves, Susie.

Merry Christmas!

SUSIE Merry Christmas Lindsey...

LINDSEY *(Sees* **RUTH** *is there. Beat. Joins her.)* Ruth Connors.

Merry Christmas.

RUTH Christmas.

An outdated religious ceremony.

Beat.

LINDSEY Okay.

RUTH Heard you made gifted.

LINDSEY heard *you* made gifted.

RUTH It'll probably be *lame.*

LINDSEY probably

RUTH I dreamt about Susie.

HOLIDAY *barks.*

LINDSEY I don't

RUTH I was inside the earth and Susie walked over me in the cornfield.

I called out to her but my mouth filled with earth.

LINDSEY I have nightmares about rats nibbling the ends off my hair.

RUTH That's

LINDSEY I miss her more than anyone will ever know

HOLIDAY *barks, he goes for the gloves.*

Holiday!

Leave them!

HOLIDAY *runs off, whining.*

SAMUEL *finds* **LINDSEY.**

SAMUEL Hi, Lindsey

LINDSEY Hi

RUTH Bye

RUTH *exits.*

SUSIE *It's Samuel Heckler!*
He's so... *(Cool...!!!)*

SAMUEL Merry Christmas Lindsey!!!

LINDSEY Okay.

SAMUEL Okay.
I heard you made *gifted.*

LINDSEY Yes
Caden signed me up.

SAMUEL Me too.
We'll both be going to Gifted Camp.
So
Here...

Holds out small box wrapped in blue paper.

She looks at it.

Are you going to open your gift?

LINDSEY Okay

She wrestles the bow off it.

SAMUEL My mum did the ribbon for me

LINDSEY She sure ties a *tight* bow.

A small box.

SAMUEL Open it.

LINDSEY I'm scared.

SAMUEL Don't be

He puts his hand on her forearm.

SUSIE *(feels it in heaven…)* Wow!

Franny!

FRANNY *appears…*

Lindsey cute boy touches her in *the cornfield*

And *I* feel it here!

An amazing discovery of sensation…

FRANNY Well…it's Not The Deal but…

Merry Christmas!

SUSIE This is *news*

FRANNY You wanted to grow up…

LINDSEY Wow

It's…

SAMUEL Half a heart

Gold, right?

He reaches inside his shirt, takes out the other half, also on a chain.

I split my heart…see…?

SUSIE Lindsey…

You'd *never* have told me any of *this stuff*!

Both **LINDSEY** *and* **SUSIE** *simultaneously react.*

LINDSEY *moves towards* **SAMUEL.**

Kisses him.

SUSIE *feels it in heaven.*

Oh this feels like...!!!

Into memory.

RAY You're *beautiful*, Susie Salmon

SUSIE Am I?

RAY Yes.

Come on, let's cut English with Mrs Dewitt

SUSIE I like Othello

RAY So do I...but...

It's *condescending twaddle* the way she teaches it

SUSIE Okay...

RAY Laurence Olivier in *black make-up*!

SUSIE so *lame...*

RAY Dewitt just makes the *whole* tragedy into

A sort of *Black Like Me* version of The Moor!!!

SUSIE *Right!!!*

RAY I've seen all the RSC productions...

SUSIE ...Why do you talk like that?

RAY I'm from England.

SUSIE It sounds so cool.

RAY I'm going to kiss you.

And a first kiss...

SUSIE If I'd known this was going to be the sex scene of my life I'd have prepared a bit...

They both slightly miss each other's lips...

They try again.

Better...

They try again.

Get it right.

RAY When you kiss me I see heaven

Out of memory.

SUSIE Ray!

Stay with Me!!!

RUTH *in the cornfield.*

...Finds the gloves.

RUTH Susie Salmon

I think you're near somewhere...

(very noble...) I'll wear these for you

Puts them on.

SUSIE How's *that* going to help????

17. Ruth and Ray...

Snow falling...

RAY *with thermos...*

Meets **RUTH** *with gloves and battered book...*

RAY Hello Ruth Connors.

RUTH Welcome to the cornfield!
It's *freezing*!

RAY I prepared tea and have it in my thermos here

RUTH No thank you
"I am terrified by this dark thing
that sleeps in me;
All day I feel its soft feathery turnings, its malignity"

RAY What?

RUTH Plath.

RAY Who?

RUTH Sylvia Plath

RAY ?

RUTH Only the most significant poet of our genera/tion...

SUSIE Shut *Up*!
Three's a *crowd*!

RAY Are you going to Susie Salmon's memorial service?

RUTH I didn't know there was one.

RAY I don't think I'm going.
I don't think people want me there after...

RUTH The police

Beat.

RAY I kissed her

SUSIE I kissed you back.

RUTH Do you want some lip balm?

SUSIE/RAY *No!*

RUTH *Here*

I have *tons* of them.

You can/ keep it.

SUSIE You're *so* lame!

RAY Have some tea.

RUTH *coffee's* my beverage

RAY Susie was great.

Do you think they'll find him?

RUTH I *guess* so.

We're like one hundred yards from where it happened

RAY I know.

Do you ever think about her?

RUTH All the time.

SUSIE You do???

RUTH Sometimes, I think she's lucky, you know.

I hate this place.

RAY Me too.

This is just a temporary hell, not a permanent one

She's in heaven

If you *believe* that stuff

RUTH You don't?

RAY I don't think so, no

RUTH I do

I don't mean *la-la* angel wing *crap*

But I *do* think there's a heaven

SUSIE Ruth, there *is*

Ruth Connors

You've just gone from

Weird

To

kind of... *Special* for me

RAY Is she happy?

SUSIE No!

RUTH It *is* heaven, right?

SUSIE Right!

RAY But what does that mean?

RUTH Well, as my dad would say

It means she's out of this *shit-hole.*

RAY *and* **RUTH** *dissolve as...*

SUSIE Well, sometimes heaven's a *shit-hole* too!!!

JACK *and* **RUANA** *appear...*

18. Jack and Ruana

SINGH *house...*

JACK Mrs Singh

RUANA Something to drink...?

JACK No.

I want to talk to your son Ray.

RUANA No you don't.

You *know* he's at school.

You want to talk to *me*.

JACK He wrote her a *love* note.

RUANA Yes

JACK I wanted to thank him for that.

I wish *I* had.

Told her I *loved* her.

RUANA She knows that.

SUSIE Yes Dad, I *know* that.

JACK But your son *did*

RUANA Yes

They stare at one another.

JACK You must have driven the policemen nuts.

Beat.

I imagine it's been hard /for Ray

RUANA *No* I won't allow that.

You have lost a daughter and come here for some purpose.

And waits...until...

SUSIE Tell her Dad

JACK I *know* who killed her.

Beat.

He lives in the neighbourhood

Beat.

RUANA What are you doing about it?

JACK Investigating all leads

RUANA And my son...

JACK Is a lead

There's *nothing* to link this man to the crime but my *suspicion...*

RUANA What is the man's name?

JACK George Harvey.

Beat.

The green painted house.

RUANA *decides...*

RUANA Ray will be here soon.

I will let you talk to him.

Beat.

Mr Salmon

I would do exactly what you are doing.

I would talk to everyone I needed to.

I would not tell too many people his name.

When I was sure

I would find a quiet way

And I would *kill* him.

19. Abigail and Len Fenerman...

SALMON *house...*

ABIGAIL *(She is drawing with* **BUCKLEY***'s crayons... An orange poodle. A blue horse undergoing shock treatment...)* Jack wants to talk to you.

He went over to Ray Singh's house

FENERMAN There's no point.

Ray Singh's got a whole roomful of kids to prove his alibi is *airtight...*

ABIGAIL I'm sure you're too busy to wait

FENERMAN No

Beat.

You remind me of my wife

ABIGAIL *She* can't draw either?

FENERMAN She wasn't much of a talker when there was nothing to say.

A yellow ball of sun.

A brown house with flowers outside the door... pink, blue, purple...

ABIGAIL You used the past tense.

FENERMAN She died soon after we were married.

Beat.

She killed herself.

JACK Abigail!

ABIGAIL I'm sorry

FENERMAN I am too. About Susie. Really.

They stare at each other.

SUSIE What are you *doing*?

Don't look at *him*!

But **ABIGAIL** *does...*

Rush to the sink!

But **ABIGAIL** *doesn't.*

Stare down the hole and look into the earth!

I'm down there waiting!

Warning...

Mum... I'm up here *watching* you!

You need to help Dad *find* me...

JACK *enters the space.*

ABIGAIL *and* **FENERMAN** *stop looking at one another.*

FENERMAN I hear you went to see Ray Singh.

JACK Yes I did.

Detective Fenerman...

We really need to talk...

What?

You wanna come through to *my study...?*

But there's a weirdness in the room...

FENERMAN *follows* **JACK** *into his study...*

SUSIE What's going on?

Franny!!!... (**FRANNY** *appears...)*

Something strange is going on!!!

FRANNY It looks like *adult* stuff

SUSIE Well, I don't like it!

Get somebody!

FRANNY You wanted to grow up, Susie...
Well...*this* is grown-up stuff!

SUSIE Not *this* way!
I just want to see her doing mum stuff
not *this* stuff
This is *sick*!
We need to stop this!
Do something!
HELP!!!
Anybody!

20. Grandma Lynn Hits Town

LINDSEY/BUCKLEY Grandma/ Lynn

SUSIE Not *her*!

But **GRANDMA LYNN** *is ready, she's in...*

JACK Lynn

ABIGAIL Mum.

LYNN O Lord...

Decides...

Jack y
We need some stiff drinks
Buckley sweetie you're getting so *tall...*
Hello Dog...
Lindsey...
You need to get yourself starved down, honey
Baby fat is *jus-t* another way to say *ugly...*

LINDSEY *flounces off.*

ABIGAIL *Mother!!!*

JACK Lynn
This is a different house than last time you were here.
I'll get you a drink
But I ask you to respect that

As he heads drink-wards.

LYNN Still handsome as hell, Jack!
How is he?

ABIGAIL Coping.
But it's hard

LYNN Is he still muttering about that man having done it?

LINDSEY Man. What man...?

And eavesdrops harder...

JACK Lynn

Seven and seven or a martini?

LYNN What are you having?

ABIGAIL/JACK He's not drinking/I'm not drinking

LYNN Now *there's* your problem.

Abigail

You need *help*

your face...!!!

It's bag o magic time!

Everybody warms up as...

BUCKLEY Bag o magic time!

Bag o magic time!

LYNN Kids, get your mother over here.

I'm doing a makeover

ABIGAIL Oh no...

LINDSEY Oh yes, the bag o magic

LINDSEY *sidles back into the room...*

HOLIDAY *grabs the make-up bag, family chaos ensues.*

JACK Abigail

ABIGAIL She may get you to drink but

JACK I'm not drunk

ABIGAIL You're smiling

LYNN So *sue* him

ABIGAIL *bursts into tears.*

LINDSEY *walks out.*

Susie was a good girl, honey
Just like *you*
Now lift up your chin and let me have a look at those
enormous bags/ under your eyes...

ABIGAIL *Mother!*

SUSIE Lindsey?

LINDSEY *in* **SUSIE***'s room looking at clothes.*

LYNN *joins...*

LYNN Hello? Knock knock
I thought I heard you in here

Beat.

LINDSEY What do *you* want?

LYNN I need help with this zipper
Can you get that?

Gets **LINDSEY***'s help through sheer force of personality...*

It's *one* of the reasons you need a *man*
You can't do this stuff *yourself*

Beat.

LINDSEY I want to wear something of *hers.*

SUSIE *Not* my poncho!

LINDSEY I've forgotten what she looked like.
I mean her neck you know
Did I ever look at it?

LYNN Oh honey come here

LINDSEY *doesn't.*

SUSIE My neck's *really* nothing special, Lindsey...

LINDSEY I need to look pretty

LYNN You *are* pretty

We'll find a nice outfit in here

Well, we'll *try*...

And, magically...

What do you think?

It is inspected...

SUSIE My *favourite* church dress

LYNN Where did she get *this* sack?

SUSIE Black-watch wool with a Peter Pan collar!

(it is flung back as...) okay...

I liked it mostly because the skirt was so big and you can draw your knees up under it

LYNN *(another dress)* Voila!

LINDSEY It's so short

LYNN I'm shocked *shocked* at your mother.

She actually let the kid get something *stylish*

And helps **LINDSEY** *get into it as...*

SUSIE It's actually *borrowed* it's *Clar/issa's...*

LYNN There.

What do you think?

LINDSEY I look

LINDSEY/SUSIE So grown up.

LYNN You need this.

She takes out a lipstick...

Applies it to **LINDSEY**'*s lips.*

...this finishes off the outfit

And...

it doesn't look like it but...

it's *armour*

LINDSEY Who was the man you asked Mum about?

LYNN What man?

LINDSEY You asked Mum if Dad was still saying *that* man did it.

What man?

LYNN He's called

Mr Harvey

LINDSEY Mr Harvey?

JACK Everyone downstairs and ready in *ten* minutes!

LYNN No time for rouge

This puts a little life into them...

And she pinches **LINDSEY**'*s cheeks.*

Come on kid.

Exits.

LINDSEY Mr Harvey

21. Susie's Memorial Service...

RUTH *sings, alone a song in the style of* ***"I'M GONNA BE (500 MILES)"**** by The Proclaimers.

A memorial service which settles around them...

FENERMAN *there...*

ABIGAIL Detective Fenerman.

JACK Thank you for coming.

Will you join us?

FENERMAN Thank you.

I just want to be in the vicinity...

JACK We appreciate that.

FENERMAN *looks at* **ABIGAIL** *...*

FENERMAN You okay?

ABIGAIL *looks at him.*

Abigail...?

ABIGAIL *nods.*

LYNN *sees this... comes between them as...*

LYNN You are...?

ABIGAIL Len.

Detective Fenerman

---

* A licence to produce THE LOVELY BONES does not include a performance licence for "I'M GONNA BE (500 MILES)". The publisher and author suggest that the licensee contact PRS to ascertain the music publisher and contact such music publisher to license or acquire permission for performance of the song. If a licence or permission is unattainable for "I'M GONNA BE (500 MILES)", the licensee may not use the song in THE LOVELY BONES but should create an original composition in a similar style or use a similar song in the public domain. For further information, please see Music Use Note on page iii.

LYNN I'm the evil mother!

Come stand here, Abigail...

Next to *Jack*...

SUSIE being dead makes you very popular

There's a poem by Ruth...

It's about *me*

RUTH I

golden-haired dog

following your trail

through dew-wet grass

My mind

lobster

clawing through its deep sea cage

My heart

telescope

looking for you in your dark sky

Everybody sings.

MR HARVEY *appears on the periphery...*

LYNN *(looks around during the singing... arrested by* **HARVEY**'s *figure... to* **LINDSEY**...*whispers...)* By the door.

That's him...

Isn't it?

LINDSEY *turns round.*

Sees **HARVEY** *there.*

LINDSEY Yes

Looks at him...

that's Mr Harvey...

HARVEY *looks straight at* **LINDSEY**.

SUSIE *(sees him...)* That look of wild bottomless lust

Lindsey don't *talk* to him!!!

don't *go* anywhere with him!!!

LINDSEY *faints.*

ABIGAIL *Lindsey!*

All gather round **LINDSEY** ...

Commotion.

Parents worry... **FENERMAN** *hovers...* **LYNN** *observes... variously.*

Lindsey! Get her some water...give her some space give her some air...it's the girl's sister!!! Jack...hold her...get her / on a chair...

JACK Lindsey, what happened?

What did you *see*?

Did you see *Susie*????

LINDSEY He was here

JACK Who?

LINDSEY/SUSIE Mr Harvey!!!

JACK *stands up, turns to look for* **MR HARVEY**, *but he's vanished.*

22. A Baseball Bat...

JACK Bastard

You murderous bastard

He opens a cupboard, rumples...

Takes out a baseball bat.

"find a quiet way..."

He turns off every light...

"and kill him"

SUSIE Dad...

His feet crunch as he goes through the cornfield...

Dad...shhhhh...

JACK *picks his way stealthily.*

JACK *stops.*

SUSIE *stops.*

Both listen.

Both hear the crunch of other stealthy feet.

JACK *(whispers...)* I know you're here.

I'm here for this.

He's trembling.

nobody's awake but you and me.
You've killed your last little girl Mr Harvey!!!

Is about to bring down the bat.

A horrible crunch.

Blackout.

23. Bones Moving Around...

Lights on...

JACK *in chair. Injured leg.*

ABIGAIL, FENERMAN, LINDSEY, LYNN ...

FENERMAN What were you doing in the cornfield, Jack?

At *night,* Jack

Was this one of *your walks*?

JACK *Yes*

FENERMAN You can't go around attacking teenage lovers in cornfields

JACK It was dark.

I thought it was *Him.*

FENERMAN Two courting teenagers, Jack!

JACK I'm sorry

FENERMAN You could have harmed two innocent kids.

They could have killed you instead of... *(gestures to his injured leg...)*

You must *stop* stalking George Harvey

You must *stop* making calls to us about him.

JACK I *know* he did it.

FENERMAN *Bridal* tents and *your* intuition are not *evidence*

Things have got to move on

JACK You're stopping your investigation of him

FENERMAN There's *no* evidence, Jack

JACK *stands up...*

Jack...

JACK somebody help me upstairs...

LINDSEY *and* **LYNN** *go to either side of him.*

FENERMAN Abigail he's got to *stop* this

ABIGAIL I know.

Beat.

Len...

why did your wife kill herself?

FENERMAN She was unhappy

ABIGAIL Why was she unhappy?

FENERMAN I don't know.

It's what I think about when I'm not thinking about things like your daughter's murder.

ABIGAIL *(smiles)* Say that again

FENERMAN What?

ABIGAIL My daughter's "murder".

Nobody says it.

To have it said *out loud*

Say it

FENERMAN Your daughter's murder

ABIGAIL Thank you

And she kisses him on the mouth.

I *know* why I want to kill myself.

FENERMAN Don't kill yourself.

FRANNY *watches. Tries to comfort distraught* **SUSIE.**

24. Things to Count...

HARVEY *in his house.*

SUSIE He keeps things to *count*

She watches as **HARVEY** *examines...*

The heel of a shoe...

A wedding ring

A pair of glasses

As...at Gifted Camp...

An eraser in the shape of Mickey Mouse

A small bottle of perfume

Plastic bracelet

My Pennsylvania keystone...

To remember.

25. Gifted Camp

*...***LINDSEY** *and* **SAMUEL** *are poring over an assignment paper...*

RUTH *and* **RAY** *...awkward and separate some way off...*

LINDSEY *(reading)* "Here is your last assignment at Gifted."

SAMUEL "We want you to solve a murder..."

He stops.

LINDSEY It's okay.

I'm okay.

It's just a lame *exercise...*

Let's do it.

SAMUEL "We want you to solve a murder...

In a locked room

There is a dead body on the floor by a table plus two chairs, cooker and ice box...

The one window and the door are locked.

On the floor, a small puddle of water...

What happened?

Remember...

Most murders are easily solvable

because somebody always makes a mistake

overlooks something crucial

leaves a clue

or a trail of clues.

LINDSEY it's about the puddle of water...

small puddle.

Why *small*?

SAMUEL How little water do you need to drown/ somebody...?

LINDSEY Drowning's too/ obvious...

SAMUEL /There's no sink/ table / two chairs

Rain?

LINDSEY Windows locked /doors locked /

...Icebox!

The only other /source of water

SAMUEL *Frozen* water...

Ice! the puddle's melted ice...

LINDSEY Why ice?

RUTH *(lobs in from her place at the outer perimeter...)* It's an icicle!!!

SAMUEL sharp and pointed which the murderer's

LINDSEY/SUSIE hidden in the ice box!!!

SAMUEL you come up behind them

stick it in...

here...

guy...

LINDSEY dies

RAY *(lobs in from his place at the outer perimeter...)* Ice at thirty two degrees...

Human brain typically at 98.6

Ice melts.

LINDSEY Murder weapon...gone!

SAMUEL But... You forget to wipe up the puddle!

We Got You!

Exiting.

LINDSEY Yeah but who's the/ murderer?

SAMUEL how'd he get out of/ the room?

RUTH It's a "Locked Room Brain Cell Stretcher".

They just want to know we can *hypothesise*...

SAMUEL Lindsey...

you okay...?

LINDSEY yep.

just thinking...

SUSIE Just thinking...

26. A New Investigation Team...

LINDSEY The cops think you're nuts.

JACK "*There's no basis* for an arrest Mr Salmon..."

all they can say is "no evidence"

Without *evidence* and *a body...*

We've nothing to *move on*"

Do you need to throw up...?

LINDSEY *(shakes her head...)* Just thinking...

What would be a "basis"?

JACK Something to link him to Susie...

LINDSEY If he had something of hers...?

SUSIE My Pennsylvania keystone, Dad!!!

He collects *trinkets...*

LINDSEY So you would want to be able to get in his house...

JACK I feel I'm standing in an erupting volcano

LINDSEY Daddy

go rest, okay?

LINDSEY *goes to stand watching* **HARVEY***'s house.*

"Most murders are easily solvable

because somebody always makes a mistake

SUSIE because they're not as smart as you, Lindsey...

LINDSEY overlooks something crucial

leaves a clue

or a trail of clues..."

SUSIE Lindsey!

No!

Don't go in there!!!

Lindsey!!!

FRANNY When the dead are done with *the living*

The living can go on to *other things...*

SUSIE What about the *dead*?

Where do we go?

FRANNY *doesn't answer.*

Where do *we* go?

FRANNY *doesn't answer.*

You're *no help*!!!

LINDSEY *starts walking towards the utter blackness that is* **HARVEY***'s house.*

SUSIE, *terrified, runs to the edges of her heaven.*

FRANNY Susie...

you're *dead...*

SUSIE I DON'T CARE!!!

HARVEY *stands up, as if anticipating...*

Lindsey *wait*

FRANNY *(calls after her...)* THAT'S *NOT THE DEAL*!!!

But **SUSIE** *joins* **LINDSEY** *at the entrance to* **MR HARVEY***'s house.*

LINDSEY Just *do* it!

SUSIE I'm coming with you!!!

27. Two Salmon Girls Outside the Harvey House...

The **HARVEY** *house...its structure.*

Within it...

A straight chair.

Here and there...dollhouses in various states of completion...

LINDSEY *...in her sweatshirt, number five soccer shirt beneath...outside...staring at the house...*

SUSIE *starts drawing as...*

SUSIE Same floor plan as *our* house Lindsey.

He brought my blood in here on his clothes and skin...

he has a straight chair

where he sits and

designs dollhouses...

and

watches *you*, Lindsey

LINDSEY *breathe.*

And slightly flexes her made-strong arms...

SUSIE *(***LINDSEY** *takes a breath... knocks on the door)* Right Lindsey

You need a story...

in case he's *here*

LINDSEY *(rehearses...)* Hello Mr Harvey...

I was chasing a *kitten*

SUSIE Good!

LINDSEY It was gray/ it was *fast*

SUSIE *Detail! Motive!*

Good!

LINDSEY *(knocks again as...)* It ran towards your house
I followed it without thinking

Waits.

No one answers the door.

okay he's out

And she starts scoping the house...

SUSIE Try the basement!

LINDSEY Think!

Takes off her sweatshirt, wraps it round a foot...

Revealing number five soccer shirt...

SUSIE My clever *gifted* sister!!!

LINDSEY *kicks the glass in.*

A muffled cracking...

Waits to see if this raises anybody...

LINDSEY *climbs in.*

Stands, frightened...

Yes we're in.
LET'S GO

LINDSEY *is rooted to the spot...*

SUSIE *circles desperately...*

SUSIE We need to *get moving...*
MOVE!!!

But **LINDSEY** *is rigid with dread.*

Lindsey

remember...

when I pushed you into the *really cold river*???

Into memory.

Family photo...

Various.

Not too deep,/ kids!

They can't swim, Jack!

Me Too!

Me too!

Wuff Wuff Wuff

Etc.

BUCKLEY *makes for the water...*

He is stopped. Just.

HOLIDAY *panting as...*

one

two

three...

Go!!!

SUSIE *pushes* **LINDSEY** *into the river.*

Out of memory.

LINDSEY *can move again...*

YES!!! ...now...

Up

LINDSEY *mounts the stairs...*

You can do it!!

SUSIE *darts into the next room.*

LINDSEY Susie!!!

I saw your *back*!!!

Wonderful sister breakthrough!!!

FRANNY Susie *Stop this NOW*!

You're pushing too *hard* on *the In-between*!

You're *scaring* her you idiot!!!

SUSIE Deep breaths

Good

LINDSEY *does strength exercises.*

Good

LINDSEY Okay

Clues

A car pulling up.

SUSIE Lindsey...

it's a car...

LINDSEY Mr Harvey

SUSIE Franny!

Help!!!

FRANNY I can't!!!

A car door slams shut.

She gets holds of **SUSIE**, *restraining her.*

28. Another Salmon Girl

FRANNY has SUSIE who is a ball of fear and dread...

SUSIE I can't bear it.

We *have* to help her, Franny.

FRANNY Then leave her alone.

SUSIE I *can't*!!!

FRANNY You *must*!

It will be better for *you*...

It will be better for *her*.

Look

Lindsey is older than you now...

You need to *trust* her

They watch.

HARVEY lifts his head.

Something's odd...

What?

Inside his house...

LINDSEY sees the bedside table in a circle of light.

LINDSEY goes towards it.

LINDSEY finds the sketchbook.

Lifts it up and...

Turns the pages.

LINDSEY *dollhouses...*

MR HARVEY *silently opens his toolbox.*

Gets out, silently, a tyre wrench.

LINDSEY *turns to the last page.*

(reads) "Stolfuz cornfield"

Stares at it.

Got you!

HARVEY *at bottom of the stairs.*

LINDSEY *holds her breath.*

HARVEY *stands still, feeling the atmosphere.*

LINDSEY *rips out the page.*

HARVEY *hears it.*

Looks up towards where **LINDSEY** *is...*

HARVEY *ascends.*

LINDSEY, *desperate...searches for a weapon, somewhere to hide...anything...*

HARVEY *can move again...*

Ascends...

He reaches the room as **LINDSEY** *smashes into the bushes.*

HARVEY *runs to the window.*

LINDSEY *stumbles, rolls, runs.*

HARVEY *sees...*

HARVEY *It's a girl*

Five!

Number five soccer shirt

Lindsey Salmon.

Lights out.

Interval

ACT TWO

29. A Structure...

LINDSEY *runs breathless into her home...*

JACK, ABIGAIL, LYNN, SAMUEL... *all but* **ABIGAIL** *examining the torn page...*

LINDSEY it's something he *built* in the *Stolfuz cornfield*

LYNN *and* **JACK** *examine the sketch...*

look...

JACK Oh my God it's like a *trap...*

LYNN You went into that man's house???

JACK You're a *very brave girl...*

SAMUEL You should have called *me...*
I'd have come with you.

ABIGAIL You *broke* into Mr Harvey's house?

LINDSEY I wasn't alone.

Beat.

Susie was with me.

This stops everybody in their tracks.

Susie was *with* me!

JACK *overjoyed and vindicated.*

JACK You *hear* this Abigail?

SUSIE You *hear* this, Mum?

LYNN Okay Jack, just...

LYNN *anxious, watching* **ABIGAIL.**

ABIGAIL I have to go pick Buckley up.

LINDSEY Don't you even want to *look* at this, Mum?

ABIGAIL I don't know what to say.

Your grandmother is here.

Samuel is here.

Your father is *listening* to you.

I have *shopping* to do

A bird to cook

No one seems to realise we have a *family* a family and *a son* and I'm *going out...*

LYNN *walks* **ABIGAIL** *to the door.*

LYNN Abigail

ABIGAIL No!

Exits.

JACK You believe me now

LINDSEY Yes, Daddy.

Beat.

Dad...

I think he saw me.

JACK *(phone)* Detective Fenerman please.

Beat.

Please...this is *urgent.*

JACK *waits on the phone as...*

ABIGAIL *arrives in another space with* **BUCKLEY.**

30. Heaven Grows...

SUSIE my heart *aches*

FRANNY I know

SUSIE My mum and dad are... *(she can't finish the thought...)*

FRANNY Your mum and dad are *on earth.*

You're *here.*

It's time to be *here.*

Susie...someone wants to meet you...

Summons **FLORA.**

Beat.

Sound of wind...

Beautiful olive tree appears...

A girl appears.

Twirls in a circle in her own heaven.

She sees **SUSIE.**

FLORA HERNANDEZ hello

I'm Flora Hernandez

Delaware 1963.

He only wanted to touch me...

but I *screamed.*

SUSIE You're so small.

FLORA I'm eight.

the others are on their way

SUSIE Others?

FLORA My Friends!

LEAH FOX *appears.*

LEAH FOX hello

I'm Leah Fox

I'm from Bucks County, Pennsylvania.

I'm twelve!

He killed me very quietly.

Under a highway on-ramp

WENDY RICHTER *appears.*

WENDY RICHTER I'm

Wendy Richter

Connecticut 1971

I'm thirteen!.

I was waiting for my father outside a bar...

Mr Harvey came past and saw me and...

Unlucky Thirteen!

The three **GIRLS** *slowly take places around* **SUSIE***'s heaven somewhere...*

SUSIE Susie Salmon

Pennsylvania 1973

Unlucky *Fourteen*!

I was...

GIRLS We know

We've watched you from *our* heaven

Beat.

FRANNY Some friends for you.

With

Shared interests.

How's that feel?

SUSIE *attempts to push the boundaries, it no longer leads to a hell.*

SUSIE My heaven feels bigger

FRANNY Good

GIRLS Good!!!

SUSIE Wider somehow

And she looks up from her hands...

FRANNY Good.

GIRLS NEATO!!!

FRANNY What's happening...?

SUSIE *(looks at the olive tree...at the* **GIRLS** *...)* Our heartache is pouring into one another

GIRLS *nod or smile.*

GIRLS That's because we're *friends* now!

WENDY RICHTER With Shared Interests!!!

They all giggle.

FRANNY Nice...

SUSIE *(***GIRLS** *nod and smile...)* Like water from cup to cup...

LEAH FOX Isn't it *NEATO*???

They all giggle.

FRANNY *very* nice...

why don't we all get to know more about our new/ friends...

Earthly police walkie-talkie sound distracts **SUSIE.**

SUSIE Something's happening...

FRANNY Your new friends Susie...

SUSIE *(they look towards her...she hovers, can't decide then)* they're going to question Mr Harvey!!!

YOU LOT made me nearly *miss this*!

ABIGAIL *(to* **BUCKLEY***)* do you want to play?

There's a pile of buildable stuff...child-friendly...

Build something...

While I shop?

BUCKLEY Can I?

SUSIE Mum!

ABIGAIL Do you really want to, honey?

BUCKLEY yes.

SUSIE Mum...they're going to catch/ him!

ABIGAIL Be good!

SUSIE Mr Harv/ey...

ABIGAIL I'll be on the lower level near Wanamaker's...

And watches him start to assemble something as...

SUSIE You need to *see* this!!!

31. Burying...

HARVEY *(examines the sketchbook. Turns pages to where... tear where the page is missing...)* She's taken the Blueprint of *my den!*

WENDY That's *him*!

OTHER GIRLS That's Mr Harvey!

FRANNY Oh Girls *Please!!!*

SUSIE *(to her new gang)* My sister Lindsey! Found a vital piece of evidence and she *trapped* him!

LEAH/FLORA/WENDY *mixed together as...*

FLORA She's clev/er!

LEAH She's trapped you Mr/Harvey!!!

WENDY Susie's sister's *got* you now!

SUSIE *Yes*...the *cops* have *the evidence* now Mr Harvey!

HARVEY You thieving little bitch!

SUSIE We've *got* you!

GIRLS We've *got* you!

HARVEY *very frightened.*

Arranges his trophies in some sort of weird pattern.

SUSIE My Pennsylvania keystone engraved with my initials by my father

FRANNY Susie...what did I /just say

LEAH Those look like my glasses...

FLORA That's my Mickey Mouse eraser!!!

WENDY THAT'S MY BRACELET!!!

SUSIE What are you doing with them????

All the trinkets are in a structured order...

HARVEY *hides them inside a dollhouse.*

HARVEY Keep calm go clear George go cool George
You thought ahead you thought /ahead

LEAH What's that?

WENDY What's he doing now?

FLORA Where's he putting our things?

SUSIE Oh, they'll look there Mr Harvey!!!

HARVEY *(hides the knife in the dollhouse roof)* Just in case just in case

SUSIE Your knife will be murder exhibit one!!!

HEAVENLY GIRLS YES!

WENDY Your knife will be murder exhibit one!!!

HARVEY *(pocketing the keystone)* My good luck charm
I'll keep you.

SUSIE Oh yes and it will lead them straight back to me!!!

HARVEY *moves doll house to a discreet place.*

HEAVENLY GIRLS *(following him)*

WENDY What's he doing?

LEAH Where's he taking all our stuff?

FLORA I'm frightened

FRANNY Susie these girls do not need to be remind/ed of...

Radio static.

At the mall...

FENERMAN *shadows* **ABIGAIL**... *watches her looking at items...*

COP *(on the walkie-talkie)* Detective Fenerman.?

Put a call on all channels for Detective Fenerman

We need Detective Fenerman. Any clue where Fenerman is.. ?

HARVEY *(picks up his sketchbook)* Now...what am I going to do about *you*...?

Beat.

COP *arrives.*

Where's Detective Fenerman?

My home has been broken into.

COP We're trying to locate him, sir...

HARVEY I don't wish to press charges against that poor girl.

She didn't *take* anything

COP She *did* take something, Mr Harvey...

Holds out evidence bag...

The last page of the sketchbook...

It's a drawing of the Stolfuz cornfield...

As he examines the page...

And a sort of *structure* in it...

COP *stares at* **HARVEY.**

Like an underground prison or something...

In the mall, **FENERMAN** *brushes his hand across the back of* **ABIGAIL**'*s shoulders.*

She turns...

He is going.

She follows him as...

SUSIE That's where he murdered me and everything

That structure

All stare at **HARVEY**, *who has, all this time, been staring at the drawing...*

HARVEY Oh the poor girl!!!

I'm so sorry...

She's got this *all wrong...*

Let me show you what this is

Opens his sketchbook.

There

See how similar it is to *this* sketch...?

He lets them see this...

I was trying to figure it out...

SUSIE Don't *believe* him!

You're not going to believe him are you???

HARVEY *Honestly...*?

the *horror* of that poor girl's murder has

obsessed me...

Somewhere, in the mall **BUCKLEY** *plays happily...*

He is building a structure.

I think *everyone* in the neighbourhood

has tried to think

how they could have prevented it...

I mean

Why didn't we *hear* something?

I mean, surely the girl screamed...?

Now here

Forgive me

But

I think in *structures*

SUSIE That structure's *proof*!!!

You're *hopeless*

Where's Detective Fenerman?????

BUCKLEY *(climbs into his structure...) Fort.*

Satisfied with his fort.

He sits.

At the mall...there is a deafening thrumming of air sucked out of the mall, reconditioned and pushed back in...

ABIGAIL where are we?

FENERMAN under the mall...

Reaches out and takes off her scarf.

Then...grazes her fingers with his own.

She puts her hand in his hair, clutching it...

Abigail, what are we doing?

He brings her in closer...

As...

HARVEY And

I decided that perhaps...

Well

That the person who did it had *built* something underground...

So her cries would be *muffled...*

I'm a *maker*

I make *dollhouses...*

FENERMAN Abigail think of what you're/ doing...

ABIGAIL I'm tired of thinking.

Kiss me.

Please.

So he does...as...

HARVEY See...?

So

I tried to find *an answer* for us all...

I gave it a chimney and a shelf...

Well

That's just my habit...

I have a lot of time to myself so I was trying to *help...*

I did think I had something there

COP Then...

Why didn't you call us?

HARVEY *Honestly...*

I wasn't bringing back their daughter, was I?.

I didn't want to interfere

In the mall...

FENERMAN *and* **ABIGAIL** *removing clothing...*

SUSIE Mum!

She is stopped by what she sees.

A terrible moment..

FRANNY *takes* **SUSIE***'s hand...holds it...*

FRANNY when the dead are done with the living...

the living can go on to other things

SUSIE not *this*

FRANNY yes.

this.

COP *leaves.*

SUSIE *(it is terrible for her...)* you have *my* body...

But eventually...

as it will never become...

Mum...

She looks away from **ABIGAIL** *...and towards* **HARVEY.**

HARVEY narrow escape narrow escape

if they start thinking if Detective Fenerman starts really thinking about this...

The **GIRLS** *and* **SUSIE** *watch* **MR HARVEY** *leaving his house as...*

SUSIE Dad...

my murderer is *packing up his belongings...*

HARVEY *does...*

He is...

He's *leaving...*

FLORA I'm *frightened*!!!

The **GIRLS** *hold hands. They are all frightened.*

SUSIE *(***HARVEY** *exits...) He's getting away!!!*

Dad!!!

Mum!!!

But everybody in heaven can only watch.

And everyone on earth is too busy to notice.

Open your eyes!!!

(to **FRANNY***)* this is *hell*!!!

FRANNY no

this is *heaven*!!!

she's only trying to find a doorway...

out of her...*ruined* heart...

SUSIE I can't!!!

BUCKLEY *in his fort fires a pretend ground to air missile.*

It comes crashing to the ground.

FENERMAN *lit.*

ABIGAIL *has left her scarf.*

He picks it up.

Brings it to his face to smell her as...

32. Ignition...

Family all fractured...

SUSIE my family's about to...*ignite*!!!

FRANNY I know

SUSIE *Lindsey!!!*

LINDSEY I'm going out.
To meet Samuel.
Okay?

But nobody answers her...

LINDSEY *runs into* **FENERMAN** *arriving...*

Why do you have my mother's scarf?

Silence.

Why do you have my mother's scarf?

FENERMAN She might have left it in my car one day

LINDSEY What was she doing in your car?

Silence.

What was she doing in your car?

Silence.

Mum...?

Silence.

Dad...?

JACK He's vanished!
Gone!
That's suspicious, right?
They took fingerprints from his house...

that's got to mean you're suspicious, right?

(to **ABIGAIL***)* I won't give up!

No answer.

I know I'm right!!!

No answer.

FENERMAN There is *no evidence*

JACK No evidence

And...he's *vanished*?

No evidence is all you can say

FENERMAN without evidence and without... *a body* ...we have nothing to move on and no basis for an arrest...

JACK How could you let him just vanish???

Abigail?

Abigail...are you listening...?

ABIGAIL Yes, Jack.

JACK *exits.*

Quietly.

No, Jack.

SUSIE Grandma Lynn...help! Mum!

LYNN *is watching* **ABIGAIL.**

LYNN Your father had a long-term affair in New Hampshire

Her first initial was F

I never knew what it stood for.

Found a lot of options for it over the years.

Beat.

Did you know that?

ABIGAIL No

LYNN I guess I never told you
I didn't think you needed to know.

No reaction from **ABIGAIL.**

Now you *do*, don't you think?

No reaction from **ABIGAIL.**

My poor, poor sweetheart
Give me your hand.

She doesn't. **LYNN** *takes it anyway.*

Susie's death brought your father back to me
I never let myself mourn him properly.

ABIGAIL I know

LYNN Do you resent me for that?

ABIGAIL Yes

LYNN Good.
See…that's a nugget

ABIGAIL A nugget?

LYNN Something that's coming out of all this
A nugget of *truth* between us.

ABIGAIL *takes that in…*

ABIGAIL Do you know how alone I've always felt?

LYNN That's why we're talking, Abigail

But…

ABIGAIL I can't describe what I'm feeling to anyone

But…

I don't know what to do

LYNN Would you promise me not to see the man anymore?

ABIGAIL What man?

LYNN The man you're involved with

ABIGAIL I'm not involved with anyone.

Beat.

Mother...

If I needed to get away for a while

...could I use Daddy's old cabin in New Hampshire...?

SUSIE Mum you can't...

LYNN Have you been *listening* to me?

Finally...a terrible admission...

ABIGAIL How can I be expected to be trapped for the rest of my life by a man frozen in time?

SAMUEL Look what I've found!

LINDSEY It's just an old house

SAMUEL Look at the floor.

that's *tongue and groove work.*

look...

that's *cross-bracing* on the gable trim...

LINDSEY it's old

SAMUEL It blows my mind to say this

But

I think it's gothic revival...

LINDSEY I feel like I'm in a cave.

SAMUEL One day I'm gonna fix it up

SUSIE Lindsey...help me...

LINDSEY Samuel Heckler

fixer of broken things

SAMUEL You smell of soap.

And they kiss...

33. Some Advice...

Singing starts up.

SUSIE Aaah

FRANNY What?

SUSIE My head's throbbing
Sky's darkening

LINDSEY something's going on in the cornfield

Candles appear...

JACK It's December sixth
They're having a ceremony for Susie.

LYNN O Lord... People from all over the neighbourhood

LINDSEY Listen!

They listen.

There is singing...

JACK *goes to join the singing.*

Candle.

FRANNY It's that night again

SUSIE Yes
I've been here a *year*

FRANNY *Earth* Year

SUSIE I *know,* Brain Central!

LINDSEY *Mum* let's go...

ABIGAIL No.
That's done for me

LINDSEY What's done?

ABIGAIL I don't believe she's waiting out there
I don't think lighting candles and doing all that stuff
Is honouring her memory

LINDSEY Okay

ABIGAIL There are other ways to honour it

LINDSEY Like what?

ABIGAIL Like *living*!
I just want to *live*!

Beat.

A shaming admission...

I want to be more than *a mother*

LINDSEY I understand.

Beat.

I want to be more than *a girl.*

Beat.

Are you going to leave us?

ABIGAIL I won't leave you
Come here, baby

LINDSEY *does.*

You are doing so well, Lindsey
you are keeping your father alive.

Cuddles and rocks her as...

I won't leave you.

34. Kissing Outbreak...

DEAD GIRLS *pass* **RUTH** *on her way to the memorial...*

WENDY Hello Ruth...

LEAH Hi Ruth Connors...

FLORA RuthRuthRuthI'mFloraHernandez!!!!!!

They see each other.

Brush past her.

She feels their hands on her cheek, shoulders...

RUTH Hello...?

SUSIE Ruth!

Can you *see* us?

Can you see *me*?

RUTH *senses them all around her until...*

RUTH Time for the experiment.

RAY Okay.

SUSIE Ray and Ruth are *Big Friends now*?

They go to kiss.

You're just *Friends*!!!

They kiss.

RUTH I don't feel anything

RAY I don't either

SUSIE *Good!!!*

RUTH Did you feel something when you kissed Susie?

RAY Yes

RUTH What?

SUSIE *What?*

RAY That I wanted more

SUSIE *I* wanted more!

RUTH And sex?

RAY/SUSIE We hadn't got that far.

RUTH We could keep trying

RAY I thought you liked girls

RUTH Here's the deal

You pretend I'm Susie

And I will too.

RAY You're so screwed up.

They smile.

RUTH It's just an *experiment*

They kiss again.

RAY Shit!

RUTH What?

RAY I think I feel something!

SUSIE *No!*

You don't!!!

ABIGAIL Have you ever made love in the ocean?

JACK No.

ABIGAIL Neither have I.

Let's pretend it is the ocean and that I am going away and we might never see each other again.

As...

LINDSEY *and* **SAM** *embrace, it gets sexual, they wrap themselves around each other...fall to the ground, roll over and over entwined, making love until...*

SAM I'm sorry

LINDSEY Don't be sorry.

SAM I'll stop.

LINDSEY Don't stop.

SUSIE And

My sister sails away from me

To a place I'd never been.

In the walls of *my* sex

There's horror and blood

In *hers*

Windows

I want *to go to sleep*!

Tell me *a story* Mum...

35. Persephone...

Into memory...

ABIGAIL *is remembering...*

Bedtime...

ABIGAIL *has a book of Greek myths in her hands...*

ABIGAIL once upon a time
there was a little girl called Persephone

SUSIE *smiles.*

She knows who Persephone is...

So do **THE GIRLS**.

They all wish for and get a pomegranate...

SUSIE one day
she went for a walk into a field
and a
hand came up out of the earth
and

ABIGAIL It was the King of the Underworld

SUSIE *hides in* **ABIGAIL.**

and he took her down
under the earth.

Beat.

She looked *everywhere* for her little girl...

It is unbearable.

Lights a cigarette.

Everybody waits for the story to continue...

Until...

once upon a time

there was a little girl called Susie

one day

she went for a walk into a field...

and her mummy looked *everywhere* for her little girl

but

although she looked high and low

she never found her

because

her little girl was *dead*

and her mummy *knew* this

and she knew it was time to *stop looking*

And she gets up and as **SUSIE** *watches, leaves...*

SUSIE The next day

she *(***ABIGAIL** *departs as...)*

My mother leaves

JACK Hey, Ocean eyes

Where'd you go on us?

ABIGAIL The sea.

The sea

And disappears...

LYNN Jack...

I'd like to make myself available to you and the children

I know I'll be no replacement for...

but...

I will contain my drinking until...

Terrible sacrifice.

After five o'clock

Even more dreadful sacrifice...

What the *hell*

I'll stop altogether...

JACK You don't need to do that

LYNN Thank God for that!

Okay... I now live...

Shudder.

here...

Music in the style of ***"PSYCHO KILLER"*** **by Talking Heads starts.*

Beat.

Where are you going to put me?

Beat.

JACK Susie's/ room.

SUSIE She can't have that that's *my* room!!!

FRANNY Let *them* work it out for *themselves...*

SUSIE *(***FRANNY** *offers her a pomegranate)* It's still too early.

FRANNY Not down there it isn't.

---

* A licence to produce THE LOVELY BONES does not include a performance licence for "PSYCHO KILLER". The publisher and author suggest that the licensee contact PRS to ascertain the music publisher and contact such music publisher to license or acquire permission for performance of the song. If a licence or permission is unattainable for "PSYCHO KILLER", the licensee may not use the song in THE LOVELY BONES but should create an original composition in a similar style or use a similar song in the public domain. For further information, please see Music Use Note on page iii.

Down there... Time just...*flies...*

And it does.

RUTH/SAMUEL/LINDSEY/RAY *in their separate rooms etc...*

SUSIE Ray you got so handsome!

He's packing books for college...

(to **FRANNY***)* I've missed stuff!

FRANNY It happens

In his old Shakespeare **RAY** *finds.*

Marking the last act of.

SAMUEL We could just work on our house.

LINDSEY We're gifted. We *have* to go to college

RAY *The Tragedy of Othello The Moor...*

A photograph book marker... **RAY** *studies it...*

Susie

Susie Salmon

SUSIE don't throw me away...

And **RAY** *puts it somewhere safe to take as...*

RUTH I think I've got second sight.

I see dead women and children everywhere. I need to be open and free to reach them...

SUSIE Reach *me*!

RAY I've been reading my pre-med literature...

a lot of of care home patients

tell doctors

that they see someone standing at the end of their bed at night...

SUSIE See *me*!

Somebody!!!

But nobody sees her...

She looks at the other people on earth...

JACK *has a book open, but is staring into space...* **HOLIDAY** *at his feet.*

Dad!

Nobody's looking for Mr Harvey!!!

FRANNY They're getting on with their lives without you.

But **SUSIE***'s not listening...*

SUSIE Then *I'll* have to look for him!

GIRLS *look up.*

RUTH *sees them looking.*

We'll have to look for him

FRANNY *NO!!*

SUSIE *We'll* have to hunt him down!!!

GIRLS Yes!!! Yes! Yes Yes!!!

SUSIE Where is Mr Harvey now?

FRANNY This isn't The Deal!

Girls THIS IS ABSOLUTELY OUT!!!

GIRLS *disagree...*

36. Old Clues...

FENERMAN *with evidence box.*

SUSIE *and* **THE GIRLS** *hover round him...*

Provide...

Exhibits...

Thoughts.

Ideas...

Study the incidents board...

SUSIE Detective Fenerman.
With my mother gone...
you've nothing to do but
Look *again* at the evidence...

And he does.

Think!

He picks up.

My jingle-bell hat

Tinkle of bells.

Drawing of the cornfield

He examines the sketch...

think, Detective Fenerman
Mr Harvey's disappearance

He is thoughtful.

anything...????

He seems to think of...

He rises.

Goes to.

FENERMAN Dig

SUSIE And

Dig again

FENERMAN this time

SUSIE/ FENERMAN the *whole* corn field

COP *digs in another part of the space...*

Earth forked up until...

COP Hey!

He holds an old Coke bottle.

old Coke bottle

COP *gives it to* **FENERMAN.**

SUSIE My last drink on earth...!!!

now we're getting somewhere!

FENERMAN *turns the Coke bottle over in his hands...*

FENERMAN Let's get this to the lab...

Hands it on...

two clear prints...

SUSIE match it with the one off the snow globe...one is

FENERMAN Susie Salmon's...

SUSIE the other...

off his doll house...

FENERMAN *Harvey*

The Murdered Girls dance with joy.

37. Susie and Mr Harvey Watch the World Spin...

SUSIE *joins* **MR HARVEY** ...

SUSIE Mr Harvey's living wild, aren't you?
sleeping in your dilapidated car, aren't you?
he's just killed a waitress.

HARVEY *(counting money...)* twenty-five, twenty-six, twenty-seven, twenty-eight, twenty-nine dollars

SUSIE that's her tip money you're counting, right...

HARVEY good.
That's good.

He stands up to pocket the money.

His back is sore from sleeping in a car...

In his pocket he feels something. Pulls out keystone. Examines it.

SUSIE Hello keystone!
are you missing home, Mr Harvey?
you should see it Mr Harvey...
a family of five live there now
three little girls
Lindsey babysits for them when she's on vacation...
they've painted it lavender...
they've put in a pool

Sound of excited girls splashing...

In the neighbourhood...

Everybody is doing stuff...

JACK *is looking at the photograph of* **ABIGAIL** ...

HOLIDAY *at his feet, asleep...*

RUANA *and* **LYNN** *are playing cards for matches...*

BUCKLEY *is doing a homework assignment...*

JACK Hey Ocean eyes...

I dreamed about you last night...

Looks closer...

look how Susie captured you

so *sad...*

HARVEY *has had terrible nightmares of fives, tinkling bells, murder, girls...*

HARVEY five

Why five?

SUSIE our *whole* neighbourhood think it was you who killed me...

Detective Fenerman's looking for you

Cops all over the North East Corridor are coming up with evidence about you...

HARVEY bells!

why bells?

HARVEY *hears, from his nightmare...the sound of* **SUSIE***'s jingle-bell hat...*

He shakes his head to try to clear it of the sound...

SUSIE the trees between our house and yours have gotten so tall

Buckley's getting tall too

He wants to be Wolverine

because /Wolverine

BUCKLEY Wolverine/ has a skeleton made of the strongest metal in the universe

and can heal from any wound overnight...

BUCKLEY *shows* **JACK** *what he's written...*

Dad I wrote a story...

JACK *(reads)* "Once upon a time there was a kid named Billy.

He liked to explore. He saw a hole and went inside but he never came out.

The End."

The **HEAVENLY GIRLS** *become* **HARVEY**'*s worst nightmare.*

FLORA I'm Flora Hernandez

LEAH Remember me?

WENDY Unlucky Thirteen!!!

HARVEY I don't want to think about *you*!

It was an *accident*!

You were *an accident*!

I got mad and couldn't stop myself!

OTHER GIRLS *surround him with instruments of torture.*

I don't want to remember any of you!

Chucks all other trinkets...but holds on to the keystone.

SUSIE Remember me!

38. A Visit From Mr Harvey...

SUSIE He's taking Interstate ninety five
Where are we going?

He looks at the landscape...

He looks again...

She recognises...

HARVEY the sinkhole!

Looks around again...

old safe with no key...
just *there...*
where those two are standing...
I've got unfinished business here...
you put something in that safe...
you put something in that safe...
what did you put in that safe?/
Get that safe!

At the sinkhole...

He's disturbed by...

RUTH They're bulldozing the whole wasteland area...

SUSIE *drain* the sinkhole
open the safe
find my body parts...

RUTH concreting over it

SUSIE *(defeated)* No

RAY Our childhood is vanishing before our very eyes...

Beat.

It's *spooky* round here, Ruth

RUTH Yes I feel it.

RAY That sinkhole's always been dangerous

RUTH *moves to...*

Ruthie, that's close enough!!!

Let's go

RUTH *(looking down into the sinkhole)* This place is *totally* spooky

She can sense something...

something's *here*

RUTH *straining to see* **SUSIE.**

Ray...?

RAY What?

RUTH Do you ever think where Susie Salmon's body ended up?

HARVEY Susie

He drops the keystone.

RAY Yes. I think about her all the time. Come on.

And **RUTH** *sees her...*

RUTH Susie!

Hey

SUSIE *Odd* girls find each other in the *strangest* way.

RUTH I've written poems for you.

SUSIE I know you have Ruth

You've always been *poetic*

Beat.

You look *great* in black

RUTH *looks.*

RUTH *(sees the* **GIRLS***)* Who are you?

Sees **MR HARVEY***!*

In his car!

Mr Harvey...

RUTH *faints.*

SUSIE *(cries out)* Ruth!!!

SUSIE *falls to earth.*

Suddenly, shockingly.

39. Falling Out of Heaven

FRANNY *appears at a rush.*

FRANNY Susie!

Susie!!!

Where Are You????

SUSIE I'm *in* Ruth's body!!!

FRANNY Susie you must *not do this*

This is Absolutely Forbidden!!!

HARVEY *approaches.*

SUSIE I'm...

In Ruth!

FRANNY That *isn't The Deal*!!!

SUSIE The *marvellous* weight weighing me down is

The weight of *a human body*!!!

RAY *appears...runs for* **RUTH** ... **HARVEY** *backs away. No one cares.*

RAY Ruthie!

What *happened*?

RUTH *(opens her eyes)* Try it

Looks at **RAY***.*

Electric shock moment.

RAY *Wo!*

RUTH What?

RAY You've changed.

Something's changed

SUSIE Kiss me

RAY What?

SUSIE Kiss me.

RUTH Pretend I'm Susie
Just as an experiment

SUSIE Don't you want to?

RAY *(strange but…)* Yes.

And kisses her.

SUSIE When you kiss me I see heaven

RAY *(looks closely into her eyes)* You're not Ruth.

SUSIE No

And waits until he finally realises…

RAY *…Susie…?*

SUSIE *(nods)* I've watched you both for years
I'm here right now

He touches her.

She touches him.

RAY But you'll be gone soon

SUSIE I think so, Ray. Yes.

RAY Don't go.

And **SUSIE**, *in* **RUTH**, *and* **RAY** *kiss and embrace more deeply…*

SUSIE I touch every part of him
hold him in my hands
that part of him that Mr Harvey forced inside me.

Inside my head I say
"gentle"
and then
"man"

40. The Smell of Smoke...

LYNN *(sniffing the air...)* Foreign cigarettes! Got to be...

Meets **RUANA**, *smoking...*

Ruana!

Are you having a party?

RUANA My *husband's* having a party

LYNN And you're out here!

RUANA This is a *crazy* place we both live!

LYNN Call this *living*?

RUANA No, I call it "a temporary hell I am enduring until the instant my son graduates med school and all this will be merely a dreadful *memory...*"

LYNN Do you have another of those...?

RUANA Absolutely, Lynn, yes.

41. Raised Voices...

JACK *and* **BUCKLEY** *between scarecrow made from* **SUSIE***'s clothes...*

HOLIDAY *hovering...*

SUSIE What are you doing with my clothes Buckley?

JACK No!

Take them down!

No you *cannot* have them!

BUCKLEY Why not????

JACK What do you want them for?

BUCKLEY To stake my tomato plants!

It's a bird scarer!

JACK They're *Susie's*

BUCKLEY I know they're Susie's.

Now *I* need them!

You have to *choose.*

It's *not fair*!!!

You act like Susie was *yours only.*

Mum left because you wouldn't *choose*

US!!!

JACK *clutches his chest...*

Falls.

LYNN, LINDSEY, SAMUEL *etc. rush to him.*

LYNN Oh God...

it's a heart attack...

he's

LINDSEY Dad!

BUCKLEY Dad/dy...?

SAMUEL I've got him I've got him!!! Mr Salmon wake up can/ you hear me...

LYNN Jack... What happened?

SAMUEL I'll call the para/medics!

BUCKLEY Daddy...?

LYNN Lindsey *get a blanket*!

LINDSEY Buckley go sit on the chair just go sit on the chair...

...

LYNN Somebody needs to ring your mother!!!

LINDSEY No!

JACK Let go

Let go

Let go

Abigail?

SUSIE *comes close...kneels by him...*

Susie...?

SUSIE Daddy...

She takes his hand.

He feels it somehow...

if you want to die...

do it.

just do it.

Beat.

it's okay...

Beat.

I'm here
You'll be with *me.*

BUCKLEY Please don't let Daddy die...

A moment. Unresolved.

ABIGAIL *approaches as the family assemble round* **JACK**...

LYNN Abigail *thank God!!*

ABIGAIL How is he?

LYNN He's asking for you...
Abigail...

Beat.

He's asking for Susie too

ABIGAIL *comes to the centre of the family...*

LINDSEY Mum

ABIGAIL Lindsey

Beat.

How is your father?

SAMUEL He's not in the greatest shape

LINDSEY Mum

ABIGAIL I said I would never leave you.
But I did.

They look at each other.

Then...

Hello Buckley

BUCKLEY *(whispers:)* FUCK YOU.

ABIGAIL Buck...

will you look at me?

BUCKLEY *glares his fury at her.*

ABIGAIL *in to* **JACK**...

JACK Hello Ocean eyes

ABIGAIL Jack

JACK Look what it took to get you back

ABIGAIL Was it worth it?

JACK I fell in love with you again while you were away

The photo is there.

I love you... Queen of the Amazons.

ABIGAIL Out loud I say to people I have two children

Silently... I say three.

I couldn't stop thinking it was because when I got pregnant I didn't want her...

JACK It doesn't work like that, ocean eyes.

Beat.

Someone came into the room.

I think it was Susie.

ABIGAIL I see her everywhere

I see her hair but it doesn't match her face...

I see her body then it doesn't move like her...

JACK Come here.

She goes close to him.

42. A New Old House

SAMUEL *brings* **LINDSEY** *into a structure…*

LINDSEY It's gorgeous

but it's *still* an old wreck and…it's *still* falling to *bits*

SAMUEL Basic structure's sound.

look…

Oriel windows…

I love you

LINDSEY I know

SAMUEL No, I mean I *love* you

I want to *marry* you

And I want us to live in this house

I'm fixing it…

I'm mending all the broken stuff…

That hideous hideous college shit is over

Marry me and I'll make this house gorgeous.

Okay?

LINDSEY Okay

SAMUEL Okay?

LINDSEY Okay!!!

Samuel Healer

mender of broken things

HOLIDAY *finds the keystone.* **LYNN** *picks it up.*

43. The Lovely Bones

SUSIE These are the lovely bones that have grown about my absence

She walks round, through...

The connections

That happened after I was gone

Stops.

Moves away.

Realises.

I think I can hold the world without *me* in it!!!

And climbs to heaven where...

FRANNY well...*hallelujah!!!*

44. The Icicle Drops

SUSIE Manchester.
Maine.
Sometime later on earth

MR HARVEY Coffee

SUSIE He still looks as ordinary as ever
There's a teenage girl playing her Walkman

A girl, humming along.

HARVEY *follows her.*

They stand in the snow.

HARVEY Long ride

GIRL Uhuh.

HARVEY Are you travelling alone?

SUSIE Above them
A long and plentiful row of
icicles

GIRL Creep

She walks away.

Icicles fall.

Hit **HARVEY,** *who pitches forward.*

SUSIE It is weeks before the snow melts
And they find him
It's like the perfect unsolved murder

It is evening in both heaven and earth.

A beautiful radiant sunset.

The dogs arrive.

Among them...

Holiday...?

It is.

Holiday!!!

HOLIDAY *is polite but suspicious...*

I'm Susie
I'm the little girl you slept beside...

Joyous reunion...

Then...

Dogs, including **HOLIDAY**, *biff off to do dog stuff...*

to everyone on earth...
I wish you all a long and happy life.

Lights down.

End of Play

ABOUT THE ADAPTER

BRYONY LAVERY

Her play *Frozen* won the TMA Best Play Award, the Eileen Anderson Central Television Award, was produced at Birmingham Rep, then the National Theatre, then on Broadway where it was nominated for four Tony Awards. *Stockholm*, for Frantic Assembly, won the Wolff-Whiting Award for Best Play of 2008. *Beautiful Burnout* for the National Theatre of Scotland and Frantic Assembly received a Fringe First at Edinburgh, before productions in the UK, New York, Australia and New Zealand. *Dirt* was nominated for the Charles McArthur Award for most outstanding play or musical of 2013, Washington DC.

Recent work includes: *The Believers* (Frantic Assembly); *Queen Coal* (Sheffield Crucible); *Treasure Island* (National Theatre); *101 Dalmatians* (Chichester Festival Theatre); *Brideshead Revisited* (York Theatre Royal/ETT); *Our Mutual Friend* (Hull Truck/City of Culture 2017) and *Balls* (One Year Lease/Stages Theatre Houston and NYC). She is a Fellow of the Royal Society of Literature, an honorary Doctor of Arts at De Montfort University and an Associate Artist at Birmingham Repertory Theatre.

ABOUT THE AUTHOR

ALICE SEBOLD

Alice Sebold is the bestselling author of *The Lovely Bones* (now a major motion picture) and *Lucky*, both of which were #1 New York Times bestsellers. In 2008 her novel *The Almost Moon* was published. Born in Madison, Wisconsin, Sebold grew up in the suburbs of Philadelphia and attended Syracuse University, as well as the University of Houston and the University of California, Irvine. She now lives in California.

Other plays by BRYONY LAVERY
published and licensed by Concord Theatricals

Frozen

Treasure Island
(by Robert Louis Stevenson)

Other plays by BRYONY LAVERY
licensed by Concord Theatricals

A Wedding Story

Lightning Source UK Ltd.
Milton Keynes UK
UKHW021626160421
382087UK00007BA/543

9 780573 116865